THE GOOD FIGHT

I WILL CONTINUE TO

PATRONIZE THIS ESTABLISHMENT

IF IT IS INTEGRATED

(This card prepared under auspices
of University Religious Council)

*Life Lessons
from a Chicago
Progressive*

THE GOOD FIGHT

DICK SIMPSON

 **Golden Alley Press**
Emmaus, Pennsylvania

In this work I have recreated the events, locales, and conversations as accurately as possible from my memories of them. The details all derive from my recollections, retold in a way that evokes the meaning and essence of what transpired. In some instances, I may have compressed events. To maintain their privacy, I changed minor identifying characteristics and details of some individuals.

Golden Alley Press
37 South 6th Street
Emmaus, Pennsylvania 18049

www.goldenalleypress.com

Golden Alley Press books may be purchased for educational, business, or sales promotional use. For information please contact the publisher.

Printed in the United States of America

The Good Fight / Dick Simpson. -1st ed.

Library of Congress Control Number: 2017956477

ISBN 978-0-9984429-4-5 *print*
ISBN 978-0-9984429-5-2 *ebook*

Front cover photograph:
© 1971 All rights reserved. Distributed by Tribune Content Agency, LLC

Back cover photograph:
© Roberta Dupuis-Devlin, UIC

For all those in my generation
who fought publicly for democracy and justice
and for integrity in their personal lives.
And to those who come after us
who will pick up the torch.

CONTENTS

FOREWORD

AUTHOR AND ORAL historian Studs Terkel wrote a preface for my book *Rogues, Rebels, and Rubber Stamps*. Studs is gone, but I'd like to think he would agree that it serves just as well as the forward for this book:

> Dick Simpson was one of those reform aldermen and political opponents who got under Boss Richard J. Daley's skin. In 1971, he got Daley so mad that the mayor-for-life almost had a stroke right on the podium. I remember that moment as a choleric mayor aimed his roundhouse punches in the manner of W. C. Fields at that "college perfesser," Dick Simpson.
>
> Alderman Simpson was Daley's enemy because he represented the little people of Chicago and he organized a ragtag group of political opponents to challenge the omnipotent Daley and the Great Chicago Machine. . . .
>
> Having tried most of my working life to give voice to the voiceless, I am delighted to discover new and previously unknown tales . . . which everyone in Chicago thinks they know. . . . [M]aybe someday the little people will retake and reshape their own local governments. The struggle for democracy and justice is too important to be left in the hands of the politicians.

– Studs Terkel

PREFACE

I HAVE LIVED in tumultuous times.

During the turmoil of wars, recessions, scandals, impeachments, economic growth, new media, and political struggle, I have often had a front row seat. At the midlevel of politics, government, social movements, and institutions like universities, I know how the sausage is made, because I've been a sausage-maker.

As a media commentator, I've tried to help shape the stories, to interpret them and tell others what it all means. As a professor, I've had the time and the official duty to ponder these events, to figure out at least some life lessons from everything I've seen. I've tried to rally the public to achieve more civil rights, justice, and democracy.

In *The Good Fight*, I attempt to tell the truth about my life, including some details kept private until now. For although I have sought to live an honorable life, I, like all mortals, have fallen short. Wherever I have done well, and especially where I have failed, I would like what wisdom I have gained to flow into the world. To help us all in the good fight.

Dick Simpson
Chicago, IL
September 2017

THE GOOD FIGHT

Part I

Formation

It was a simple idea: we would stand in line in front of movie theaters and ask to buy a ticket. If you were a white kid like me, you would say, "I'd like a ticket for me and my (black) friend here." At most theaters in Texas in 1960, blacks could only enter through the back door and sit in the balcony. So the teller would refuse to sell us a ticket. In response, we would calmly walk to the back of the line. When our turn came around again, we would ask the same question.

Our songs and protest signs made clear to bystanders and potential movie-goers what was happening. Ticket sales plummeted.

As far back as the late 1930s, protesters had been using sit-ins to integrate lunch counters, cafeterias, and diners. In the 1950s, a sit-in at a Texas courthouse led to the reversal of the state's Jim Crow laws. In 1962, a young Bernie Sanders helped lead a sit-in at the University of Chicago to protest the campus's segregated housing policy. The stand-in movement at the University of Texas, Austin, was our original contribution to the cause.

When word of our stand-ins got out, other students began spontaneously joining us. The movement created its own momentum as our numbers swelled and media coverage increased. Our stand-ins eventually led to the integration of movie theaters across Texas and the entire country.

Demonstrators in front of a theater, Austin, Texas, 1960

1

TO CHANGE THE WORLD

Saul Alinsky, the father of community organizing, was right. It's best to start off a campaign with success.

A MUFFLED BANG. Flying shards of stained glass. We ducked for cover, then raced to look through the shattered window into the alley.

The pipe bomb had ricocheted off the leaded window and exploded in a stairwell below, chipping cement, knocking out bricks, and blowing shrapnel for 25 yards. The young Texans that had thrown it were long gone.

The blast in Austin that November night in 1960 shook the first planning meeting of what would eventually become part of Texas's own civil rights movement. A few dozen of us had been meeting in the Austin Student YMCA-YWCA to plan desegregation demonstrations. We had heard about the sit-ins that college students in other southern states were holding to integrate lunch counters. Our twist on the idea was to use stand-ins to integrate movie theaters – first on the Drag across from campus, and eventually in the whole state.

I was new to the University of Texas, having come there only two months earlier from an unhappy freshman year at Texas A&M. I joined the student meeting because I believed in full integration – not just

5

desegregation. I supported full equality between blacks and whites.

Like all 60s activists, we believed we could change the world. We were black, white, and undeterred by the hate we faced. Uniformly naive and idealistic, we felt immortal and a bit self-righteous. Our view of justice recognized no shades of gray. We were unencumbered by responsibility or worry that demonstrating could get us fired from our jobs. We had no children to provide for. Our parents were far away. We were invincible. We didn't really believe that we could be killed or jailed for demonstrating for justice in segregationist Texas.

We called ourselves Students for Direct Action, SDA. Unaffiliated with other national organizations like the Southern Christian Leader Conference (SCLC), the Southern Nonviolent Coordinating Committee (SNCC), or Students for a Democratic Society (SDS), we were simply the local face of the movement. Our leaders, people like Houston Wade, Casey Hayden, Chandler Davidson, and Brad Blanton, rotated from week to week. But in truth, we were all leaders. Each night, whichever SDA member arrived at the demonstrations made sure they were run nonviolently and that the classic civil rights

Clipping from a local newspaper, November, 1960

songs, with our own verses added, were sung as we stood in line at the theaters demanding freedom for all.

At dusk each night, between 50 and 100 students, both black and white, would head out to the Texas and Varsity theaters on the Drag across from campus. It mattered not what movie was showing. Our protest line at the box office was our focus.

On nights when we had enough people, we would add another picket line curbside to let passers-by know that this was a protest, not just a popular movie.

Demonstrators in front of the Varsity theater, Austin, November, 1960

Drivers hurled insults, threats, even beer bottles at us. Catcalls ranged from "I hate you," to "nigger-lovers," to "niggers pick strange places to make love." We were spit on, pushed into the gutter, and knocked down.

Brad Blanton, who chaired the meeting the evening of the pipe bomb, was quoted in the newspaper stories that followed. A gravelly-voiced man called him at home a few days later: "You nigger lovin' mother fucker, I'm going to string you up and cut your balls off."

"Well, if you do it in that order, it won't be so bad," Brad coolly replied.

Clipping from a local newspaper, November, 1960

Two Drag Theaters Refuse Protesters

The theaters attempted to counter our demonstrations with tricks of their own. When we appeared, they tried closing their box offices and selling tickets just inside the door as ushers and managers guided patrons around our demonstration and into the theater. Although this was partially successful, they still lost the business of customers who were unwilling to wait in long lines or cross our picket lines, even if they didn't agree with our efforts at integration.

When we were turned away at the box office, or at restaurants when we did sit-ins, we left a card prepared by the University Religious Council, a broader and more established group than SDA. Local theaters and restaurants collected hundreds of these cards, the carrot to accompany the stick of our demonstrations.

I WILL CONTINUE TO PATRONIZE THIS ESTABLISHMENT IF IT IS INTEGRATED

(This card prepared under auspices of University Religious Council)

The one remaining card I did not distribute in the 1960s

Early on, SDA adopted a "Statement of Purpose," a manifesto to encapsulate our feelings and idealism. We declared, without apology or equivocation, that a person's race is a totally invalid criterion of his or her worth. We declared our radical belief in total integration.

To broaden our support, SDA created a petition declaring that, after April 1, 1961, we would "attend only independent integrated theaters or integrated theaters owned by chains which are pursuing a policy of racial integration in all their affiliated theaters."

DID YOU KNOW THAT THE UNIVERSITY OF TEXAS NEGRO STUDENTS ARE STILL SEGREGATED IN MANY SIGNIFICANT AREAS OF DAILY LIFE?

- That few Drag Restaurants are open to Negro students, and some of those restaurants which are integrated require the Negro student to show his blanket tax before he can be served?

- That Negro students are barred from UT intercollegiate athletics, despite the success of other predominantly white colleges in Texas in integrating their athletic programs?

- That UT dorms are not open to Negroes, despite the proven success of other Texas colleges in integrating living quarters?

- That Negroes cannot attend Drag theaters, even though foreign language classes are often sent to certain movies as part of their official study assignments?

- That Negroes are barred from playing leading roles opposite white students in UT dramatic and musical productions?

- That Negro students have to go to East Sixth Street or farther to get a haircut, as no Drag facilities are available to them?

These are only a few of the problems which Negro students on this campus face. In the four years since UT opened its doors to Negro undergraduates, little definite progress has been made toward correcting the situation. Why is this so?

1) The actual number of Negro students is too small to constitute an adequate bargaining power.

2) Non-Negro students interested in a more humane integration program have not been able to organize into one single, well-coordinated group.

These two handicaps can now be overcome, and you can do your part to help. The Students for Direct Action Committee—a newly formed organization dedicated to peaceful, legal action against segregation—is sponsoring a petition either in front of the Texas Union or in front of the Co-Op this week (Tuesday through Saturday) protesting Drag merchants' refusal to serve Negro students. This is not an ordinary petition, however.

For by signing it, the student pledges to patronize AT LEAST ONCE A WEEK one of the University area restaurants which are totally integrated, the names of which will appear each week in the Daily Texan.

This is a legal, peaceful means of voicing your protest against social injustice. To make it effective, the student must hold to his pledge. For this reason, if you are not sincerely interested in the Students for Direct Action Committee's program, we ask you not to sign.

If the petition acquires as few as a thousand signatures, the committee will have a potent bargaining tool. Further, it will have the names of people interested in its program who can be notified of future developments. If you approve of our petition, tell your friends about it, or request some of these pamphlets at the petition booth. Now is the time to make your voice heard in favor of civil rights.

Flyer passed out by SDA on campus, January, 1961

When Eleanor Roosevelt covered our efforts in her regular newspaper column, we began to get national attention. A telegram she sent to Sandra (Casey) Cason, one of our leaders, read, "I admire so much the stand which the students at the University of Texas have taken and I particularly hope there can be a change of policy at the theater at which *Sunrise at Campobello* [a movie about her late husband, FDR] is playing."[1]

National support increased even more when Sandra, who later married Tom Hayden, convinced the Executive Committee of the National Student Association to pass a resolution commending our demonstrations and encouraging other universities to take up stand-ins against segregated theaters. SNCC later endorsed our tactic as well.

By January of 1961, allies in other states joined with us to put nationwide pressure on the large chains that owned the Varsity and Texas theaters. By August, SDA had successfully negotiated an end to the chains' policies of segregation. We had succeeded in integrating over 100 movie theaters across the nation all at once, years before the Civil Rights Acts of 1964 and 1965 passed Congress.[2]

As for the sophomore students who had thrown the pipe bomb, they were fined $200, spent three weeks in the Travis County jail, and were later readmitted to the university.[3]

Being part of the stand-in movement changed all of our lives. Most of us stayed active fighting for social justice for the next sixty years. I would go on to hear Dr. Martin Luther King, Jr. give a version of his "I've Been to the Mountain Top" speech in Chicago, and help elect the first black mayor of Chicago. Saul Alinsky was right – starting our fight with a success encouraged others to join and helped us keep the faith during the trials and tribulations that followed.

---

1 Jordan Buckley, "The Desegregation of Austin's Movie Theatres," https://www.austinchronicle.com/screens/2015-12-04/the-desegregation-of-austins-movie-theatres/

2 "The Stand-Ins," http://peopleshistoryintexas.org/standins/

3 Buckley, "The Desegregation of Austin's Movie Theatres."

In the mid-twentieth century, segregation felt different in the Southwest than in the deep South. It was equally appalling, just more nuanced. A sign was as likely to say "No Mexicans Allowed" as "No Coloreds Allowed."

Segregation showed itself in an odd sort of pecking order. White males were on top, followed by white women and children. Then came Latinos and Mexicans. Blacks came last.

But Texas had ranches and small farms, not plantations. Texas ranchers and farmers were an independent, self-reliant lot who didn't expect to be waited on hand-and-foot by servants. And many blacks in the Southwest didn't descend directly from former slaves as they did in the South. So, although they might have found themselves doing menial tasks, blacks weren't typically treated like servants. They were workers.

Blacks couldn't eat in restaurants with whites or sit with them in movie theaters. Grown black men were likely to be called "Boy." And all blacks were expected to be deferential to whites. But black women were our nannies, black men were our country club stewards, and blacks or Mexicans did our yard work for pay. There was opportunity to get to know each other as real people, not just stereotypes. But although blacks and whites knew and might even like each other, they weren't considered equals.

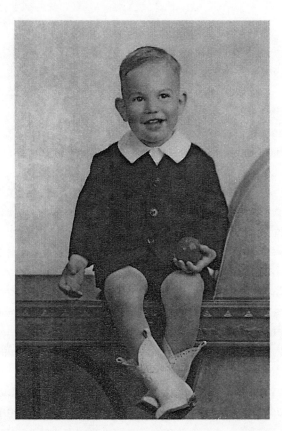

Smiling in my white boots, 1945

2

GROWING UP TEXAN

*It's tough to maintain prejudices against
someone when you're sharing a meal or
doing the same sweaty job.*

I AM SMILING in all my childhood photos. And why not? I was an only child, living the idealized white middle-class Texas life of the 1940s and 50s.

Then, before I was even three years old, World War II called my father away. Mother and I joined him in Mississippi for basic training, where Dad and I happily spent my third birthday being driven around in a jeep by his army driver. But once he shipped overseas, Mother and I returned to Houston to spend the war years alone.

When I was five, my father was discharged a lieutenant colonel and a decorated war hero. Mother and I traveled to San Antonio to meet his train, where he greeted me with the spoils of war: a mechanical songbird in a gold cage, butterflies in a glass frame, and a real German gun. But I was unimpressed.

We spent our first night together in a San Antonio hotel room. As kids will do, I knocked over a wastepaper basket. As dads will do, he ordered me to pick up the mess.

"You made a mess, Son. Now pick up the trash," he said.

Mom, Dad, and me, 1943

"No," I said, my five-year-old arms folded across my chest.

"Do as I say, Dickie Boy. Pick up the trash."

"No."

"Son, if you don't pick up the trash, I'm going to have to spank you."

"No." I said. I wasn't about to let this stranger boss me around.

Exasperated and unused to being disobeyed, Father raised his hand to me, spanking me until we both ended up crying.

Finally, in compromise, he said, "Okay, Son, let's clean up this mess together." And so we did.

Back in Houston, Dad and I slowly rediscovered each other, and peace reigned. There were just a few more spankings, the last one when I was nearly a teenager. An unknown thief had stripped some blossoms from our yellow rosebush. I protested innocence, but Dad didn't believe me and gave me a good whipping with a switch. I never learned who the real culprit was, but I did learn the pain of unjust punishment.

Texas summers were hot and humid. We did yard chores early to beat the daytime heat and played sandlot baseball in the late afternoons. Evenings were for touch football across neighborhood yards.

The roar of the attic fan kept me awake nights.

My piano teacher, Old Mrs. Unzwicker, lived just down the block. Blessed with endless patience and a love for music, she gave me nine happy years sharing her piano bench. I was no Van Cliburn, but I eventually learned to make real music. My lifelong love of the symphony began when she took me to my first Houston Orchestra concert.

We were one of the first families in our neighborhood to own a television. After dinner, the three of us would move to the den to watch *I Love Lucy, The Ed Sullivan Show,* or *The Lone Ranger.* But despite the TV, I was a reader. I was hooked on the Hardy Boys mysteries, westerns, and my favorite, science fiction.

One thing all my favorite books, TV shows, and movies had in common: heroes who worked to change the world for the better. I was that kid who believed wholeheartedly in the American ethic and in honest, trustworthy, and brave men like Abraham Lincoln, Davy Crockett, and the Western cowboys. Most of my friends were not as hooked on the Western ethos, or they got jaded later on. But I remained a true believer, and literally, a Boy Scout.

In fact, most of my boyhood revolved around the Scouts. I dove in wholeheartedly, selling tickets to the Boy Scout Circus to everyone in Dad's office building downtown, at our country club, and on our block, earning my way to New York City twice.

Headed for NYC, 1952

15

My enthusiasm and all-American looks conspired to make me something of a poster boy for the Scouts. This led to some fun photo ops, especially when I was in New York and got to meet actors and actresses – like Gloria Swanson and the radio comedian Fred Allen.

We gave Gloria Swanson a handkerchief as a gift.
That's me in the lower left corner, 1952

As beautiful as she was, Gloria Swanson couldn't compete with my excitement over meeting my hero, Roy Rogers, when he rode in the Wild West show at the Houston Coliseum. We went on Scouts Day, and sure enough, there were Roy and Trigger, doing their tricks just like I'd seen them on TV. I could barely speak when we went backstage to be photographed with him, but Roy was as friendly as could be. I learned early that movie and TV stars were people, too.

Scouting also introduced me to outdoor adventures. One summer we hiked across 100 miles of New Mexico, learning wilderness skills and Native American ways. To this day I carry a small scar just below my eye from getting hit by a spear during an intricate Native American spear dance.

When I was about twelve, I became a counselor and worked at Camp Strake all summer long. From then on, for one week each

With Roy Rogers. I'm on the left, looking slightly
star struck, 1952

summer, I was counselor for African-American Scouts. There were four
or five white counselors and 200 or so black Scouts and their leaders.
Those weeks were no different from all the "white" weeks during the
rest of the summer. Swimming together, eating together, being friends,
growing up together, we were all just Scouts.

I'm the happy boy in the back row, far left, 1954

In my teens, I was inducted into the Order of the Arrow. As part of our initiation, we stayed awake all night, fasted for a day in the wilderness, then finished with a bonfire ceremony in a hidden part of the camp. By the time I became an Eagle Scout, I had been taught honor, loyalty, and service. And it was in the Scouts that I first learned to preach.

In my Explorer Scout uniform with my Eagle, God and Country, and Silver Awards, along with Order of the Arrow Patches, 1955

Mother and I were Methodists, in a break from my Grandfather Felts, a Nazarene circuit preacher from Siloam Springs, Arkansas. We may have all kneeled together for bedtime prayers when we visited "Papaw," but we didn't absorb his fundamentalist rules against smoking, dancing, and drinking. The Jesus of my youth became just another hero in my Western pantheon.

Segregation was a given in Houston back then. Whites lived where I did, blacks lived "somewhere else." I never personally saw a black person turned away from a theater or restaurant, because they didn't even come to our part of town except as maids and yardmen. We didn't so much see segregation, as live it. But there was one place in town that I regularly experienced segregation firsthand.

We belonged to the Braeburn Country Club, a typical "whites only" establishment. Caddying was a good-paying job, so beginning the summer I turned 12, I began to caddy for my father. In every foursome, all of the caddies except me were "colored." My father may have been a bigot, but he wanted me to have the job and didn't mind that I hung out with the other caddies, whatever their color. It was hard work in muggy Houston under the hot sun, so we mostly paid attention to our jobs. But when we had time, we got to know each other, and the other caddies were accepting of me. It was an experience that none of my white school classmates had, especially not the children of the local oil barons.

While Dad played cards, I had plenty of time to kill after swimming. So, I hung around Wilson, the Braeburn Club's African-American head steward. Wilson's first name was Ed, but everyone called him by his last name – an improvement over being called "Boy." Wilson was a dignified man who, for all practical purposes, ran the club and supervised all the other "help." He and my dad became buddies over the years, but they never fraternized outside of the club.

After I graduated from high school mid-year in December, 1958, I needed a job before going to college the next fall. My father was the vice president of a company that rented the drill collars, bits, and pipes that were needed on an oil rig. The company's facility in Victoria, Texas, needed someone to maintain the equipment. Would I like the job?

After an unsuccessful two-week stint trying to sell cars – which I learned was harder than selling Boy Scout Circus tickets – I jumped at the chance. Thus I spent my last summer before college living in a motel in Victoria, maintaining drilling equipment. Whenever we got the call that something had gone wrong in an oil field, two of us would jump to load four or five tons of equipment onto a one-ton truck. Trying valiantly to keep the front wheels on the ground, I would then drive alone like a madman for 50 or 100 miles to deliver the equipment and unload it to the rig roustabouts, returning just about sunrise.

In my downtime, I devoured books about nuclear physics. It was my parents' dream that I would become a nuclear physicist, and I took their dream with me to college my freshman year.

My dad was a Texas A&M alumnus. A&M had been his escape route from hard farm life, and he loved the camaraderie of the Corps of Cadets. His Aggie ring, which I still have all these years later, was his most prized possession. Every fall for fifteen years, Dad, Mother, and I enjoyed going to the A&M football games together. We all assumed that, when the time came, I would be an Aggie just like him.

In this sheltered Texan life of mine, I never saw crime directly. Books and television shows were sanitized. I never witnessed a ghetto family struggle with poverty. I knew nothing of politics during the Eisenhower years. I had no ethnic identity; I was just an American. The fact that I was an entitled white male did not penetrate my consciousness. It was simply a given in this time of conformity in America.

But all of that changed when I arrived at Texas A&M.

Today, Texas A&M is a major university with an outstanding faculty. But when I arrived as a freshman in the fall of 1959, it was still an all-male, all-white, mostly-military student body. We looked grand, marching in parades and standing in the football stands in our uniforms. But scratch the surface, and along with its pride, honor, and traditions, it reflected the considerable anti-intellectualism present in the 1950s and 1960s. This was a military academy meant to train soldiers and military leaders, not scholars.

Founded as a land-grant college in 1871, A&M's mandate was to provide agricultural and mechanical training to young men. By 1959, when I attended, it was a second-level military academy, lacking the glamour of West Point or Annapolis. But it was turning many a farm boy, like my father, into military officers, businessmen, and engineers.

Prairie View A&M, our supposedly sister campus, was about 50 miles south on Highway 6. Like many of the all-black colleges that dotted the South and reached as far southwest as Texas, Prairie View was a coed, civilian college that provided a college-level education for blacks.

Very few of the cadets on A&M's main campus even knew Prairie View existed – we may as well have been on separate planets.

Dear Fish,

On December 3, 1959, there will be a "Fish" Class Election. Since I have been on the Aggie campus I know that I have met at least a thousand Fish buddies, and of these that several will attempt to be elected to a class office, even as I will. I also beleive that I and all of the class of '63 have a right to learn the qualifications of each candidate. Then when we meet them personally and make our own estimation of their capabilities, personality, and character we will be better qualified to vote for the good of the class. I have taken the liberty of adding my own qualifications for the office of Fish President and hope that other candidates will do the same.

PAST

1. Received the Eagle, Silver, and God and Country Awards in Scouting and through these achievements have attended Jamborees & National Conferences.
2. Chief of the Order of the Arrow in Houston (1700 members)
3. Graduated 4th in the class from Bellaire High School, Jan. 1959.
4. Was a member of the National Honor Society, National Forensic League, Junior Academy of Science ect.,ect., in High School
5. Scribe of Sam B. Cantey Jr., Chapeter Order of DeMolay.

NOW

1. President of the Fish "Y" Council
2. Fish Yell Leader when we outscored the Couger Kittens
3. G.P.R. at mid-semester was 2.18
4. Member of the Wesly Fish Fellowship and Wesly Players

Sincerely,

Dick Simpson

My campaign letter for 1959 Texas A&M Freshman class president, when I still naively believed the best qualified candidate would always be elected

REBELLION AT A&M

Opposing injustice is not without consequences.

TEXAS A&M WAS the college for me, or so I thought. My whole life had been programmed toward the moment when I put on the uniform of the Corps of Cadets.

My time as an Aggie started easily enough. Wearing the ROTC uniform, marching, drilling, learning the rules and traditions, surviving hazing, it was all part of life as a "Fish" in Company B-1. I stood stiff and proud in the back row of our company photo.

I'm in the back row, eighth from the left, in 1960

Following my parents' dream, I dutifully declared a major in physics. But scoring a D in calculus sent me to the counseling center, where an apperception test revealed that I was better suited for social work, ministry, or sociology – an early hint at my true calling.

Between Boy Scouts and church, I had been appointed to so many leadership positions that I assumed I would be a natural for 1959 Fish president. In my experience, if you were a good guy, had a good program, and made a good presentation, people would vote for you. But I quickly learned that wasn't how politics worked at A&M, or more generally in the world.

No one in my class knew or cared about my past achievements. Getting elected as Fish president was a popularity contest, and I had neglected to run a political campaign. I lost in a landslide.

In addition to my rude political awakening, I discovered something else about A&M: beneath its proud surface, it seemed to combine the worst of fraternities gone bad with the anti-intellectual qualities of a military academy of that era. This combination was anathema to me. My interests began moving in a different direction.

I soon joined the Student YMCA and the Wesley Foundation at the local Methodist Church. There, I found a spiritual and intellectual home and connection with like-minded students. In place of a popularity contest, both groups treated me as a valuable human being and fed my intellect and idealism.

I loved attending the Student YMCA-YWCA's integrated, statewide co-ed retreats. An anomaly in segregated Texas, the retreats were also attended by Prairie View A&M students. I befriended black student leaders and their pastor from Prairie View, Rev. Lee Phillips. Rev. Phillips became a mentor and friend to me, and I drove the 50 miles to visit him whenever I could. The more I got to know these students and Rev. Phillips, the more my political eyes were being opened.

We hadn't talked politics much at home. Although nearly everyone in Texas at that time was nominally a Democrat, I couldn't have told the difference between Republicans and Democrats, and I didn't have a party preference. It wasn't until a year later, on September 26, 1960, that I listened to the first Kennedy-Nixon debate as I drove to a Student YMCA-YWCA gathering. Unable to see the stubble, sweat, and clumsiness that caused Nixon to lose the televised debate to Kennedy, I just listened to the words. Based on what I heard, I decided I must be a Democrat. I decided to back Kennedy.

As my political leanings and my academic goals changed, I slowly veered from the path that my parents had intended. But the temperature in the cauldron of my freshman year was soon to increase even more.

On the fourth floor of our dormitory, a freshman decided to quit the university midyear. The seniors in his company, certain that he would squeal about being hazed contrary to university rules, convinced his fellow Fish classmates to punish him. While he was off resigning from the Corps, we all watched as they obediently tossed all his papers and clothing out of his fourth-floor dorm window. Then, in a somewhat bizarre concession to conscience, they carefully carried his record player and records downstairs and deposited them in the yard among the blowing papers and crumpled clothes.

Outraged, I wrote a scathing editorial in the Wesley Foundation newsletter, filled with brave declarations like "If this is what it means to be a man and an Aggie, I don't want to be either."

Now it was my turn to be shunned. Afraid that someone on campus would see my editorial, my fellow cadets retaliated by ostracizing me. No cadet was allowed to speak to me for weeks. Every single cadet obeyed the order; not one of them stood up to the peer pressure of the Corps. Being ostracized hurt, but my anger at the injustice to my fellow cadet got me through it.

The contrast between that level of conformity and the open environment at the Y and the Wesley Foundation was not lost on me. The event crystallized for me everything that was wrong with the Corps of Cadets, despite its vaunted history and how supposedly wonderful it was to be an Aggie.

Mercifully, the school year finally ended. In two eventful terms, I had crossed the Corps of Cadets, spoken out against injustice, and learned I could survive the consequences – lessons which would become invaluable soon enough.

My year as an Aggie in the Corps of Cadets, 1959

Growing up in the sheltered 1950s, sex was something private that happened in the bedroom, presumably only between married couples.

Dating was mostly a group activity, much tamer and less sexually oriented than it is today. Playing bridge, going to movies and plays, attending school dances – these gave us space to get to know each other and find our awkward way in the world.

We guys usually did the asking, which meant the girls had to wait to be asked. We did the driving, too, picking our dates up and delivering them safely home to their families at the agreed-upon time. If we went out to dinner, we ordered for our dates and almost always paid the tab.

Dating followed a predictable course of events; each stage had its own set of expectations. Flirting led to group dates. If those went well, a double-date might be arranged, sometimes with one of the couples on a "blind" date set up by the other. If we really liked a girl, we'd ask her to go steady and give her our class ring, which she'd hang on a chain around her neck or wrap with angora yarn so it would fit her finger.

Wedding to Mary Scott Head, September 8, 1964

4

COMING OF AGE

Be nice to the people you meet on elevators.
You never know what the future may hold.

SOCK HOPS, FANCY dances, playing bridge at the 'Y'. Double-dates with Wayne Shull, my best friend from Scouts. Each carefree high school weekend blended into the next. Bari Boden, a fiery green-eyed redhead, was my best girl until our puppy love couldn't withstand the separation of college.

A&M was an all-male environment, so we went off-campus to meet female coeds. It seems quaint now, but the rules for dating sorority women were quite strict. The young lady and I would sit circumspectly together in the sorority lounge until we stepped out for a meal or to campus events. Curfew was firm; I had to return her before the gates locked at 11 p.m. I dated a series of interesting young women until my odyssey took a starkly different turn.

At a dance with Bari Boden, 1958

First, however, I had to tend to the business of changing universities.

When I broke the news to my dad that I was leaving A&M, he took it better than I expected. As was our habit, we didn't speak directly about the change. I just made it.

The University of Texas was my best option. Switching loyalties was a challenge because UT and A&M were stark rivals, especially in football. But UT was far superior academically. Some of my friends from the A&M Student Y pointed me to the thriving Christian Faith and Life Community there. I visited it in late summer to be sure it was right for me, and moved in as soon as I transferred the next fall.

At the Christian Faith and Life Community, fifty or so of us lived together in a former motel, taking our meals communally and attending daily worship services. The radical premise of the community was that, given the opportunity, the laity could understand theology and philosophy as well as the clergy. That we could design our own worship services, understand existentialism, and affect change in our world, both individually and collectively. It was an empowering idea.

Some of the best teachers I ever had instructed us in theology and philosophy. They taught us how to teach, how to learn, and how to join into committed, intentional communities.

"*You are a free person in the midst of the 20th century.*" We repeated our mantra so often it began to sound silly. But it was the 60s. We knew we were living in an era of change, and we were free to choose what to make of ourselves. It naturally followed that we would reject segregation and that we would act on our convictions. Many of us joined the stand-ins and civil rights demonstrations off campus, walking to the nearby theaters to join the lines blocking the ticket windows.

At the beginning of the spring semester, an older student returned to the community. Fresh from his stint as an officer of the National Student Association in Philadelphia, he was worldly-wise and charismatic. I was from provincial Texas, a transfer student from a rigid military academy. I envied his knowledge and charisma, and wanted to be more like him.

At first, we were just good friends living at the community with 48 other classmates. But his affections soon fell on me, and I felt myself responding. With my parochial background, I never would have imagined this happening to me. But as we sat across from each other in his room one night, he declared that he loved me. He said I had to decide whether I loved him, and was willing to, in his words, "risk it."

I knew exactly what he meant by "risk it." To display public affection, to be anything other than completely circumspect, we would suffer at the hand of outraged Texans. But I had to admit that I was drawn to him. And difficult as it was to decide, I could not deny my feelings for him.

He taught me many things; among them was a myth about Indian warriors. A warrior can be a sun-hunter or a moon-hunter, he said, and sometimes both. The sun-hunter seeks glory in politics or their profession in the bright light of day. Moon-hunters are emotional, feeling, mystical, religious, lovers following the tricky light of the moon. Intuitive and quiet walkers, their path is less distinct, but their emotions rage high. Theirs is the path of love. The myth immediately captured my imagination. From that moment forward, I struggled to find balance while following both paths.

Our relationship ended naturally when he moved away, and this homosexual experience was never repeated. As far as I know, our relationship remained a secret known only to my future wives. I certainly did not admit it when I was an alderman or running for Congress – to have done so would surely have ended my political career. But it made me sensitive to gay rights and taught me to take risks in love as in politics.

After I graduated from UT, I moved to Indiana University for graduate work in political science and African studies. The year was 1963, and in November of that year, President Kennedy was assassinated in my home state of Texas. I learned of the shooting when I was in the middle of a national Student YMCA officers meeting at the YMCA hotel in New York City. All of my generation knows where we were when the assassination occurred; it was a turning point in our collective lives, just as September 11, 2001, would be four decades later.

I had just arrived at Indiana University when a striking young woman named Scott introduced herself to me on an elevator ride in the student union. Since we were both leaders in the Student YMCA-YWCA – I had just been elected national vice-president – we had many mutual friends. We also shared the typical values of 1960s students.

Mary Scott was tall, energetic, articulate, and easy to fall in love with. Blessed with a ready laugh, she was more socially outgoing than I was. An English major and a very good writer, she had aspirations of becoming an English or drama teacher, perhaps even a playwright. We dated for two years, and after she graduated and I received my M.A., I proposed marriage.

On September 8, 1964, we marched down the aisle of the Indiana University campus chapel. A Methodist minister married us in a simple Protestant ceremony. Bloomington was Scott's hometown, so her extended family and friends attended. My parents came up from Texas for the occasion.

Since Scott had spent her entire life in Indiana, she was anxious to see the world and had planned to enter the Peace Corps. She gave up those plans to marry me. In return, I promised her that we would indeed see the world as soon as I finished my coursework and could begin to research my dissertation in Africa.

Scott and I were soulmates – we loved poetry and music, and determined to be content to live simply on our teachers' salaries. We were liberal idealists, willing to sacrifice to achieve our personal and societal goals. In our youthful idealism, we made a pact not to have children, but to seek to change the world instead.

"Secret society 'devils' parade young initiates down the street. A Christian chief conducts the yearly ancestor sacrifice. Illiterate farmers, youths, and petty traders travel dirt roads and highways to Freetown's open-air markets abuzz with the same bantering and gossip that occupied their grandmothers. But the goods for sale today include flashlights, canned milk, and electronics. Every day, in hundreds of ways, traditional and modern life are molded into the new amalgam that is provincial West Africa."

This was the Africa I described in my 1967 doctoral dissertation.

Africa has always been shrouded in mystery to Americans. Its civil wars, coups, and epidemics have made it no more transparent now than it was during the days of slavery and colonialism.

In the 1960s, it was even more the dark continent than it is now. Most of our impressions came from the movies. But the real Africa didn't have Tarzan – most of it didn't even have tigers, elephants, or the kind of jungle we saw on the screen. Its ethnic groups had existed for hundreds of years before Westerners appeared on its shores. It had real people, filled with real hopes and dreams.

Market Town at Mile 90, Sierra Leone, 1961

5

BECOMING AN AFRICANIST

*Whether in a provincial African village
or big-city Chicago, it is our actions, not fate,
that determine our future.*

OUR STATED GOAL was to build a cinderblock YMCA facility in the town of Greenville, Liberia. The Y's broader goal was to introduce young American men to a world unknown to most people. So, in June, 1961, after tapping family and friends for travel funds, I found myself joining other college students in New York City for briefings before our 20-day trip to Liberia. On an evening off before we left the States, I wandered alone into Black Harlem to hear street-corner talks by Black Power activists. The only white man for many blocks, it was good preparation for my time as a minority white man in Africa.

During our eight-day sea voyage to Europe, we attended lectures on American foreign policy, African politics, and nationalism. Most African states had just gained their independence, and optimism was in the air. From what we were learning at the time, hope for smooth economic development and an easy transition to democratic governance was everywhere in Africa. But the reality would turn out differently. We learned that Liberia was founded by freed slaves in the 19th century, essentially as an American colony. Its founders' descendants became the "American Liberians" whose families ruled the country until a bloody civil war swept them from power in the 1990s.

Once in Europe, it took us several flights to arrive at Monrovia, Liberia. To introduce us to the country, we were driven to the miles-long Firestone rubber plantation, one of the most important sites in Liberia and source of rubber for American tires. That evening we met Liberian President William V. S. Tubman and American Ambassador Matthews. All was pomp and circumstance; there was no hint of the civil wars that would rack the nation only a few decades hence.

The next morning, we flew 175 miles southeast along the Atlantic coast to Greenville, the capital of Sinoe County. City officials and a crowd of people greeted us. As we had been taught, we gave snap handshakes to them all – a handshake that Liberians developed to show that their knuckles had not been broken by slavery. Some blacks in America later adopted the same greeting to claim their African heritage.

Greenville was named after Judge James Green, one of the first Mississippi Delta plantation owners to return former slaves to Liberia. With less than 5,000 residents in 1961, Greenville would be destroyed in the Liberian civil wars, then rebuilt to its current population of about 15,000.

In 1961, the town consisted of two dirt roads, Mississippi and John Stone Streets, lined with thatched huts made of mud brick and palm leaves, plus a few cinder block houses with tin roofs. Five or six shops sold staples like beer, cigarettes, gum, bananas, and cookies; two of the larger stores were owned by Lebanese merchants.

American institutions like the Rotary Club and the Y were an important part of Liberia's social fabric, one of the ways Liberians, like small-town Americans, climbed the social ladder and made economic contacts. When we first arrived, the Greenville YMCA existed within the home of its secretary, a far-from-wealthy man. Our task was to construct a new 52' x 38' concrete building – a major event in the development of the community.

Under construction: the YMCA in Greenville, Sinoe, Liberia, 1961

We worked from 8:30 am until lunch at 3:00 pm each day, then swam in the Atlantic Ocean or explored the town until it got dark at 6 in the evening. At night, we traveled to nearby villages to hear tribal music and watch the dancing.

Nearly every person in the town knew at least five or six of us by name, going out of their way to be welcoming and generous to us. Everywhere we walked, grownups and children waved and stopped to say hello. No one said, "Yankee, go home." When one of my friends tried to buy matches, the store owner insisted on giving them to him instead.

One of the most striking discoveries we made was how language connects us. Our group journal records that Liberians tended to use the word *one* rather than *a*, as in "That house belongs to *one* man," rather than "That house belongs to *a* man." One moonlit night, our Liberian friend Benny and a group of us were walking to a nearby village dance. As Benny sang "Old Black Joe," one of our group joined in. He then sang

"My Old Kentucky Home," which Benny had not heard before. "How may it be going?" Benny asked. The American student sang, "Weep no more my lady, oh weep no more today. I will sing *one* song . . ." Our jaws dropped. There it was! Not *a* song, but *one* song. Stephen Foster had copied the language of the slaves, perhaps the great-grandfather of Benny or some other resident of Greenville. This small Liberian town was directly connected to our American history and heritage in ways we had never imagined.

When our twenty days ended, the YMCA was not quite completed. The community finished the roof, plastering, and painting after we left, which ended up being to their advantage. Our international labor and funding had made it possible, but the new Y was now owned by the community alone.

I returned to America a little stronger, a little humbler, and more aware of how little I knew of the wider world.

Building the YMCA in Greenville, 1961

THE CUMULATIVE EFFECT of the civil rights violence in Austin, my trip to Liberia, and my studies at the University of Texas led me to a decision. I would begin my teaching career as an Africanist. I moved to Bloomington, Indiana, and enrolled in Indiana University's graduate program in African politics, one of only a handful of such programs in the country in 1963. Having finished my master's degree and my Ph.D. coursework, I immediately began my doctoral dissertation.

In my dissertation, I posited that the more socially and economically advanced an African town or country was, the more politically developed it would be. To test my hypothesis, I would need to choose an African country and understand its history, towns, and local politics.

My interest in democracy led me to choose Sierra Leone, in which I found two towns with very different dominant political parties and ethnicities. The ethnic groups in these towns had existed for hundreds of years prior to British colonization and the slave trade. I was anxious to dig back into their oral history, to fill in some of the gaps in what the colonialists had recorded.

I had promised Scott when I proposed to her that she would see Africa. So, in December, 1965, funded by a Ford Foundation Fellowship, we began our year-long African adventure.

After a briefing in Washington, D.C., we flew to Boston to meet with John Karefa-Smart, who was teaching at Harvard at the time. He was a close friend of the first Prime Minister of Sierra Leone, Milton Margai, a founder of the Sierra Leone People's Party, and Karefa-Smart himself became a later candidate for president. I had followed Karefa-Smart's political career from afar over the years, he being one of the rare Africans who, after becoming scholars at American universities, actually returned to their home countries. He would later fail in his attempts to guide the political evolution of his nation, particularly in its attempt to create a new government to end the civil war. But I found his writings and suggestions helpful in researching my dissertation.

After Boston, three weeks in London provided time for my library research while Scott and I enjoyed many plays. It was also our first experience with B&B living, during which we spent a small fortune feeding coins into our room's heater to ward off London's winter chill. A highlight of our U.K. trip was our visit with Christopher Fyfe, the great historian of Sierra Leone. We took an overnight bus through the moonlit Brontë-like countryside to his home in Edinburgh, where we climbed the worn stone steps to his flat. I learned more from his books than from his words of wisdom that day, but the three of us had a fine time drinking Scotch to excess together.

We finally arrived in Freetown, Sierra Leone, and headed up Mount Aureol to Fourah Bay College, which overlooks the capital city. Our month in the college guesthouse fell into a pleasant rhythm of mornings spent doing background research and afternoons enjoying Bristol Creme Sherry on the veranda with the other resident scholars.

Scott and I often hiked down the mountain into Freetown, greeting people with the smattering of pidgin-English Creole (Krio) we knew. It was a good time to be in Sierra Leone, a time of hope and optimism, soon after its independence. There were decent highways, a railroad, more or less reliable electricity in the cities, rich mineral deposits – including its famous "blood diamonds" – and a two-party political system. It seemed poised to become a more developed nation.

Once my library research was complete and I had interviewed a few bureaucrats at the capital, we bought a Volkswagen and drove 200 miles upcountry to Kenema, the first of the two towns I was to study. We set up housekeeping in a home reserved for white "European" managers of Forest Industry, a company that shipped old timber back to England.

It didn't take us long to realize that we needed to hire a driver and a cook. As Americans who were unused to "hired help," much less servants, having African employees required a mental adjustment; it seemed to run counter to our commitment to the civil rights movement. Nevertheless, these were necessities, not attempts to copy the lifestyle of former colonial masters.

My research required me to visit remote villages to collect oral

Kenema, Sierra Leone, 1966

histories from elders and interview chiefs to learn about traditional government, which still held sway upcountry. Our driver could find these villages and drive the nearly impassable roads. He was also a wonder with the machete, cutting down grasses and killing poisonous snakes, keeping the jungle from reclaiming our yard.

Our Sierra Leonean cook protected us from a different set of dangers. Besides cooking our meals, he boiled our drinking water and washed and ironed all our clothes – including our underwear – to kill larvae which would seriously harm the unwary.

Being a provincial capital of nearly 10,000 people, Kenema had some amenities. Every weekend we saw Italian westerns, Bollywood movies, and old Hollywood films at the movie theater. We occasionally visited the Peace Corps hostel where volunteers assigned to smaller bush towns and villages would come for respite. We sent and received short airmail letters on thin blue stationery. Since we had no radio, our sole source of news was the occasional *Time* or *Newsweek* magazine which arrived weeks after publication. After reading reports of America's

Mary Scott Simpson
AFRICAN GROUND NUT STEW

We got this recipe in
West Africa where we lived
for a year while Dick did
research for his Ph.D. dissertation on the politics of two
towns in Sierra Leone.

1 small onion (chopped)
2 T. peanut oil
1 lb. (beef) stew meat in 1"
    cubes
1 lb. can tomatoes
6 oz. tomato paste
1 c. peanut butter
3 c. water
2 t. chili powder

    Saute onion in peanut oil.
Add beef & brown on all sides.
Stir in remaining ingredients.
Bring to a boil & simmer,
covered, 1-1/2 hours, stirring occasionally. Serve over
cooked rice. Serves 4.

To this day, I still make our cook's recipe for African ground nut stew

flaming cities and race riots during 1966, I sent my dissertation advisor, Gus Liebenow, a request that he find me a job in one of the ten large cities that I listed, including Chicago. With my background in African studies and race relations, I thought I might be of some help when I returned home to the States.

Our months in Kenema were a time of intense discovery. I covered town council meetings and used social science methods to find and interview "big men" and influentials. My driver and I would travel to a village and meet with the chief – usually a rotund old man – in his home, or on the veranda of an elder. I was always welcomed, but expected to bring a small gift, typically a chicken. "What is your understanding of your town's history?" I would ask, and they were happy to answer. Sometimes I took notes, sometimes I used a tape recorder for the interviews. Later, I would transcribe the recordings and weave hundreds of years of remembered histories into a narrative. Over time, some of the influential men became my friends and informants, teaching me much about local politics.

When our time in Kenema was over, Scott and I, along with our cook and driver, moved to a smaller town named Makeni. At this northern provincial capital, we started the process all over again with equally interesting results.

As was inevitable, both Scott and I eventually suffered bouts of malaria; I had a mild case, and Scott a worse one, which recurred with a vengeance when we returned to Indiana. The anti-malaria drugs we took at least suppressed the disease while we were in Africa.

Scott working on her play, Sierra Leone, 1966

Not as easily cured was Scott's emotional struggle. To both of our surprise, while I was being busy and productive, she suffered from the isolation. Her plan, which had seemed sensible back in Bloomington, was to write a play while I worked. She wrote the play on her portable typewriter, just as she had imagined. But writing it did not overcome her growing sense of loneliness. She managed to endure the rest of the trip, but I have always regretted that we did not communicate more about her isolation in Africa.

After brief stops in Ghana and Nigeria, we returned to Bloomington. I translated my research notes into a dissertation, and my advisor indeed found me a job opening, teaching African and American politics at the new campus of the University of Illinois at Chicago, then called the University of Illinois at Chicago Circle, or UICC. There was brief time of panic when it seemed my career was to be derailed before it even started. My history professor, the only non-political scientist on the committee, refused to approve my dissertation. From his standpoint, it was a fatal flaw that, in addition to my extensive social science and analysis, I had neglected to include the history of the towns and areas that I had studied. I complied by adding a new history chapter, my dissertation was accepted, and I was granted my Ph.D. in 1968, after I had already been teaching at UICC for a year.

Although it was distressing at the time, I realize now that my professor was right to require the inclusion of the history chapter. Over time I have become keenly aware of the importance of political history and historical analysis in explaining current-day politics. In my books, such as *Rogues, Rebels, and Rubber Stamps: The Politics of the Chicago City Council from 1863 to the Present*, and *Corrupt Illinois*, with its analysis of more than 150 years of public corruption, I combine social science methods with historical storytelling to uncover the past and its effect on the present. The turn-down of my original dissertation provided a good lesson. Although I initially failed to include history in my dissertation, I have since employed it effectively to describe the present and to propose reforms to create a better future.

IN THE 1960s, both Communists and Americans believed that social and economic development automatically brought political development. They only disagreed about whether that development would result in socialism or Western democracy. If that assumption were true, it would follow that Kenema, the more socially and economically developed town, would have generated greater political participation than less-developed Makeni. Yet, I discovered that the opposite was true. Makeni produced greater political participation than did Kenema. Based upon intensive interviews of leaders and a door-to-door survey of households, I discovered that regular citizens in Makeni participated in more key decisions about developments in the town, elections, and local government reorganization than did their counterparts in Kenema.

Why did this happen? My research indicated that political development depends upon political history and political actions by leaders and citizens. Economic or social development, such as wealth or modern education, do not automatically produce political development. That is, the level of democracy is determined by the actions of men and women, not by economic determinism or the "invisible hand" of capitalism.

This finding flew in the face of the naïve – and optimistic – Western assumption of automatic and continual progress, and the belief that social and economic progress automatically bring political progress. Instead, it meant that our future depends upon our own political actions and not upon fate or economic determinism. That by our political efforts and leadership we can overcome determinism.

My empirical finding was not adopted by academia because it ran in opposition to both Soviet and American thought and writing of the 1960s, especially books on development which were meant to guide newly-independent nations. Later sad failures, like the African civil wars, and a few surprising successes would prove those theories to be false. But even with today's more sophisticated efforts at nation-building, we have still to learn the simple lesson of my dissertation: we cannot shape a people's political future from the outside, neither by military force nor economic investment. We can only provide assistance as they create their own destiny, melding traditional and modern life into their own unique amalgam.

Even though my finding would not change academic thought, I put it to use in my own efforts to transform Chicago politics. On a practical level, a lot of what I saw in Africa applies in Chicago. Our neighborhoods still have ethnic group divisions, and the person with "clout" is still, more often than not, a rotund old man. We have deeply-ingrained political histories that must be taken into consideration. We have to work hard to overcome our divisions, but our future depends on our actions, not upon fate.

Whether it was popular or not, the basic conclusion of my dissertation, that we can shape our future by means of our own political participation, would become the touchstone of my efforts to reform Chicago and change America.

At the height of the Cold War, youth and student organizations were very active. They both mimicked and tried to overcome the split between East and West, communism and democracy.

Some groups earnestly used educational and cultural exchanges to bridge the gap between cultures. Other "front groups" for Russia or the U.S. tried to use youth organizations to shape world opinion and gain ideological and political advantage.

In the Soviet Union, *Komsomol* was a youth organization controlled by the Communist party. A stopping point on the way to joining the Party, most teenagers in the USSR became members around age 14. They supported the Party by attending monthly meetings and donating free labor to construction and farming projects.

In the U.S., the Student YMCA and YWCA were not recreational programs with gyms and swimming pools. Instead, they were highly-structured organizations that tried to shape the social and personal growth of young men and women on our college campuses. With a somewhat-ecumenical religious bent, they differed from the campus ministry programs sponsored by specific faiths and denominations.

The adult YMCA/YWCA backed the American student organizations with their own programs of both recreational and civic good. Student participants were generally supportive of U.S. democracy and Christianity in the broader sense. But unlike their Russian *Komsomol* counterparts, they were generally non-ideological.

The Kremlin, 1960s

6

COLD WAR LESSONS

*Never accept the government's story
without knowing the facts for yourself.*

WHEN IT COMES to Russia, not many people can say, "I was there" during the Cold War. But because of the Student YMCA exchange program, I was able to travel to the USSR in the summer of 1963 and see firsthand the Soviet Union's vastly different history, ideology, and concept of human rights. And I met a young man who would later give his life for his political openness.

Our exchange program was co-sponsored by the U.S. Student YMCA-YWCA and the *Komsomol* (Communist Youth League). Our tour guide and "minder" was Sasha, a liberally-minded graduate student who specialized in American literature and the American novelist John Steinbeck. At a time when all travelers to Russia were required to have an official guide, and citizens were encouraged to turn in visitors who broke their strict laws, we were fortunate to have been assigned to a man only a few years older than we were, who understood and was friendly to Americans. He escorted us to the Hermitage and other museums and the obligatory cemeteries which the Soviets were particularly keen that Westerners see to reinforce the suffering of the Siege of Leningrad and the horrors of World War II.

Surprisingly, ordinary Russian citizens were quite friendly to us. They did not speak freely for fear of the KGB and local police, but they remembered the U.S.-Russian alliance against the Germans, Italians, and Japanese during World War II. While they hated and feared the American government, which they believed to be controlled by capitalistic and militaristic elements which were duping us, and they were critical of American imperialistic actions in places like Vietnam, they welcomed us individually.

Through our discussions with members of the Soviet Union of Writers and Soviet students, we discovered that even the most tolerant and liberal of Soviets and Americans still disagreed profoundly, both at the philosophical level and regarding our different government policies. No amount of friendship and tolerance could overcome the differences in our conceptions of freedom and equality.

The Soviet students accepted the Communist teaching of economic equality and the common good, while we believed in equal opportunity, capitalism, and the benefits to society at large of Adam Smith's "invisible hand." They were taught economic determinism, leading eventually to utopian democracy and the communist state. We argued for political freedom – the right to freedom of speech, religion, and an equal vote in choosing our elected representatives. Even with the best of intentions, we could not bridge these ideological gaps.

As a group, we genuinely wanted an honest exchange to better understand each other in the middle of the Cold War. However, one of our American members had aspirations of working for the CIA and foolishly decided to play junior spy. Caught taking photographs of Russian air bases out of the train window, he was taken off the train for questioning. Fortunately for him, when they developed his camera film, the Russian development process destroyed the images. Just as we were crossing the border between Russia and Romania on our way back to the U.S, he was put back on the train, a very lucky young man that his would-be spy career didn't end in a Soviet prison.

Although all of these interactions were stimulating, our most profound conversations were with Sasha, the most liberal Soviet whom we met. But Sasha paid for his open-mindedness with his life. A few years after our trip, Andy McGuire, one of our fellow American YMCA participants (who would later become a congressman from New Jersey), was able to confirm that Sasha was executed by Russia for "ideological deviations."

I DIDN'T REALIZE it at the time, but in August, 1964, I was one of many students being used as pawns in the raging international struggle between Communism and Western Democracy. Fueled by our enthusiasm, but without our knowledge or consent, our youthful zeal was co-opted in ways that I didn't recognize until years later, when I discovered that some of these programs in which I participated were covertly funded by the CIA.

At the time, there were two competing international student organizations and separate international meetings – one supported by the West, and one supported by the Soviet Bloc. Both were part of the Cold War struggles.

Two years earlier I had spent the summer at Bryn Mawr College being trained by the National Student Association to be an expert in international student affairs. I had been taught about the major student organizations and leaders in countries around the world, and equally, about U.S. foreign policy and the ideological struggles of the Cold War. Thus, I was a natural choice to be chosen by NSA to represent the U.S. at the International Student Conference.

That summer of 1964, I joined a dozen other American students in representing the United States at the International Student Conference. At the meeting in Amherst, Massachusetts, we passed various resolutions vowing peace and cooperation – even as the Cold War continued and the delegations from Latin American countries walked out in protest over various resolutions.

As I had been trained, I strongly defended the U.S. role in the Vietnam War and helped to defeat a resolution against American actions a few days after the Gulf of Tonkin incident occurred on August 1st, when President Lyndon Johnson expanded the Vietnam War effort and bombed Cambodia.[1]

Tension at the International Student Association, which ran the conference, became so great that it was disbanded in 1967. The Association was discredited when it became known that the CIA had indirectly funded it and recruited student representatives from the U.S. National Student Association to actively oppose Communist efforts to take over and direct the ISA.

MORE THAN TWO decades after my Cold War experiences, an extraordinary faculty exchange trip to Poland helped me put my 1963 trip to the Soviet Union into perspective.

In Poland in the 1980s, I learned that the Communist political science faculty members in Eastern-bloc nations had been acting as political theologians preaching Marxist doctrine. In contrast, it was the sociologists who, like their Western counterparts, were doing empirical social science on the effects of race, ethnicity, and policy, and generally escaping ideological bias – as long as they did not criticize the government. So it was with the sociologists that we had our most fruitful collaborations.

My trip to Poland taught me just how difficult the transformation of nations formerly under the control of the Soviet Union was. For instance, since all property had been state owned, all of the zoning laws and building codes had to be quickly written from scratch – the same type of systems which we had developed over more than a century. Companies had to be privatized and new management techniques implemented. There were many hurdles to be overcome

---

1   A few years later I learned of our government's deception and joined the anti-war movement.

before the beliefs and practices of the Soviet Union and the West could be harmonized and the new nations of the European Union could move forward politically and economically.

Despite the end of the Cold War, the differences I encountered in the 1960s remain evident in the tensions between Putin's Russia and the U.S. to this day. Since the 1980s, I have met every year with Russian and Eastern-bloc officials, journalists, and community organizers who come to the U.S. on exchange missions funded by the U.S. government. They are often quite interested in Chicago politics. They are fascinated to learn how we organize our local government and promote democracy, and the truth about our problems like corruption, which are all too familiar to them in their home countries.

The huge political differences that I encountered in my early travels helped me formalize my own theories of democracy and justice. I was forced to learn what at bottom – when push comes to shove – I believed. I also learned about politics and debate, but not the practical politics I would later learn in the rough and tumble of Chicago.

Part II

Hardball Politics

Finley Peter Dunne was a Chicago humorist and writer. His political cartoons were popular with President Theodore Roosevelt and became such an indicator of public opinion that they were read at the weekly White House Cabinet meetings.

Dunne's most famous character was an Irish immigrant named Mr. Dooley who spouted his opinions on politics and the social issues of his day from his South Side Irish pub. Mr. Dooley famously told his fellow Chicagoans that "A vote on the tally sheet is worth two in the ballot box," "Don't jump on a man unless he's down," and "Trust everybody, but cut the cards."

In an 1895 newspaper column, Mr. Dooley uttered his most famous quote, "*Sure, politics ain't bean-bag. 'Tis a man's game, an' women, childer, cripples an' prohybitionists'd do well to keep out iv it.*"

Mr. Dooley's quip has become a standard answer to politicians who complain about the rigors of the campaign trail. Politics as practiced in Chicago is a rough-and-tumble sport. You have to be tough to engage in it.

1968 McCarthy campaign poster from the author's collection

7

THE McCARTHY CAMPAIGN

"Politics ain't bean-bag."

JUST BEFORE LABOR Day, 1967, I was poised to begin my new job teaching African and American politics at the University of Illinois at Chicago, back when it was known as the University of Illinois at Chicago Circle. Scott and I had only visited Chicago a few times. We had no idea of the future that lay ahead of us there. But I knew this: one way or another, I was finally going to be involved in politics.

We hit the ground running. On our first day in town, we joined hundreds of people at the Blackstone Hotel for the Third Party Convention. Formally called the National Conference for New Politics, the convention was formed to find an alternative to the Democratic and Republican Party presidential candidates, in preparation for the 1968 general election. Because Scott and I were idealistic and opposed racial discrimination, the Vietnam War, and the imperial presidency, we eagerly attended.

The Third Party Convention was contentious, so most of us ended up folding into Minnesota Senator Eugene McCarthy's presidential campaign, as he seemed to be the most radical but viable candidate. Although the convention didn't endure, it became a part of the peace and civil rights movements that would later propel McCarthy's campaign forward.

When McCarthy declared his candidacy in November, I joined up. I soon heard that there were going to be strategy meetings held at a lawyer's apartment near Lake Shore Drive, right in my Lincoln Park Community. At the meeting, I criticized how they were putting together the campaign and its fledgling organization. Because of that, they naturally made me campaign manager for the 9th Congressional District on the North Side of Chicago. No one considered that I had only run college student campaigns before, rather than the hardball campaigns necessary to go up against the Chicago Democratic machine at the height of its power under Mayor Richard J. Daley.

It wasn't only me – thousands of us who joined the McCarthy campaign were young political neophytes. That's why we were nicknamed "the children's crusade." Those of us with beards and mustaches shaved them off, and we cut our long hair. We were "Clean with Gene," good, clean-cut American youth who could go door-to-door and convince Americans to vote for him in great numbers. It was magical. Just like our campaign poster declared, "He stood up alone and something happened." We stood up with our candidate, and something unprecedented happened. We unseated an incumbent president.

John Kearney was the state manager of the Illinois McCarthy campaign. John was an experienced Irish progressive politician who was also executive director of the Independent Voters of Illinois (IVI). We needed his guidance. Without the help of some "old hands" who knew the political game, we would never had made much impact. Pat and Patty Crowley were the official Illinois campaign chairmen; they had known Senator McCarthy personally through progressive Catholic organizations. They lived in a tony apartment in the iconic John Hancock building downtown. Several wealthy lawyers served on the campaign committee and began the fundraising effort. The campaign was off to a good start.

The McCarthy campaign had an amazing ability to draw in thousands of volunteers who had never been involved in political campaigns before (this would later characterize the Bobby Kennedy and George

McGovern campaigns as well). Our idealism and belief in McCarthy's platform – opposition to the war in Vietnam, to racial discrimination, and to the imperial presidency which locked everyone out of power – was the source of our willingness to work so hard. The cries of "all power to the people" resonated with all of us volunteers at some level. Hardly anyone drew a salary, even in the "staff" jobs; I continued teaching at UIC the whole time I was involved in the campaign. The power of our shared ideals was so great that many of my lifelong friendships were forged during that year.

My first act as 9th Congressional District Campaign Manager was to open an office with LaVerne Hickey. She knew more about Chicago politics than I did and became office and volunteer manager. But even with LaVerne's help, I still didn't really know what I was doing. So, I went downtown for weekly meetings with John Kearney, during which he filled me in on how to take each step to get McCarthy convention delegates on the ballot and round up votes for them in the June 11th Illinois primary.

Kearney told me to begin with a petition drive to get socialite Lucy Montgomery and publicist Herb Krause on the ballot as the McCarthy delegate candidates in the 9th District. Lucy, a colorful character who often invited peace activists and civil rights leaders to her apartment, would sometimes show up late and a bit tipsy to campaign speaking engagements. Herb was a more reliable candidate as a public relations person and peace activist, but he was not a strong public speaker. Although he was much easier to work with than Lucy, he had never run for public office. They were not ideal candidates, although they both played admirable roles in the movement for social change.

To make matters worse, we were running against two Democratic Party powerhouses. The first was George Dunne, 42nd Ward Committeeman, a former state legislator, and Cook County Board President from 1969-1990. He succeeded Richard J. Daley as Chair of the Cook County Democratic Party after the mayor's death in 1976. Dunne was one of the most powerful Democrats in the state. The second machine candidate was Jerome Huppert, a lesser political figure but still the 50th Ward Democratic Committeeman. Moreover, we were going up against the entire Democratic Party organization with all of its precinct captains, patronage workers, and loyal voters. But we were young and idealistic. We thought we could convince everyone of the rightness of our cause. We did not understand the power of the Democratic Party machine, or that this was "hardball" politics.

Nevertheless, we soon recruited hundreds of volunteers. At our regular strategy meetings and volunteer training sessions, I would convey Kearney's latest instructions and we would execute the next steps. We organized "coffees," named for the beverage usually served; although sometimes they were actually cocktail parties. The hosts and hostesses would invite their friends and all the voters in their precinct to hear our candidates speak at a social occasion in their homes, or in the party room if they lived in the many high rise buildings in our district. After discussing the campaign, one of the delegate candidates would speak. Then a coffee chair who acted as Master of Ceremonies or I would pass out pledge cards and ask for contributions of money, volunteer work in the office, or offers to do the all-important precinct work of contacting voters.

It was through this day-to-day process that I really learned the craft of politics. Because in many ways, politics is like carpentry or plumbing. You can read books about it, but it is primarily learned by doing. I also learned more about organizing people than I had learned in Boy Scouts or in college. I entered the McCarthy campaign an amateur. By the end, I was a seasoned political "pro."

The McCarthy movement, like the civil rights movement of which I had been a part in Texas, was a movement for change. Of course, in some ways it ended badly. We lost, and Richard Nixon was elected and reelected President of the United States before resigning during the Watergate scandal.

In the 9th Congressional District, we won only 20 percent of the vote, and our delegate candidates were defeated. In the entire state, we elected only four delegates out of 114 to the 1968 Democratic National Convention, and at least one of those, Adlai Stevenson III, won on his own rather than through the McCarthy campaign efforts. But the roots of political change to come lay in this "failed" campaign. It was there I learned how to weather losses, to be both a politician and a political scientist. I learned that Mr. Dooley was right. "Politics ain't bean-bag" – it is much more serious and has greater consequences than any game.

By the summer of 1968, the country was at fever pitch. Dr. Martin Luther King, Jr. and Robert Kennedy had been assassinated. Urban streets were filled with violence. Anti-Vietnam protests escalated as we watched growing numbers of U.S. soldiers return home in body bags.

It was an election year, and President Lyndon Johnson and anti-war candidate Eugene McCarthy both ran in the Democratic presidential primaries from the start. Kennedy threw his hat in the ring in March, shortly before Johnson shocked the country by withdrawing. Vice-President Hubert Humphrey entered the race after Kennedy's death, vying with George McGovern for Kennedy's delegates.

The 1968 Democratic National Convention settled into a three-way race between McCarthy, Humphrey, and McGovern.

In Chicago from August 26 through 29th, the convention would be held under the iron-fisted control of Mayor Richard J. Daley. Thousands of protesters streamed into the city to demonstrate their opposition to Daley and to a convention likely to be under Johnson-Humphrey control.

The conflicting social forces of our country were on display while protesters chanted, "*The whole world is watching.*"

Mayor Daley heckling Sen. Ribicoff at the 1968 Democratic National Convention.
L to R: Mayor Richard J. Daley; George Dunne, Cook County Board president;
Mayor Daley's son and future mayor, Richard M. Daley.

8

1968 CHICAGO DEMOCRATIC
NATIONAL CONVENTION

The times they are a'changing ... but not quite yet.

THE MINUTE WE saw televised reports of Chicago police beating up protesters in Grant Park, Scott and I hopped on the 'L' and rushed to join the demonstrators. But the jeeps, guns, and barbed wire of the National Guard turned us aside.

Welcome to Chicago, the 1968 Democratic Convention, and the police riot that accompanied it.

By now I had been promoted to Eugene McCarthy's Illinois State Campaign Manager. My responsibilities for the convention were to coordinate shuttling McCarthy convention delegates from O'Hare Airport to their rooms at the Hilton Hotel; to open our satellite office, which became a first-aid station for tear-gassed demonstrators; to arrange delegate activities; and to give out information to the press.

Campaign duties aside, once the violence started, Scott and I became swept up in this historical event. To maintain order, Mayor Daley had deployed thousands of police officers and state and federal troops, many of whom became increasingly brutal to the protesters, observers, and even members of the press as the situation spiraled out of control.

In the days prior to the convention, protesters had begun to gather in Lincoln Park along the lakefront at the Yippie-inspired "Festival of Life." Many of the out-of-town protesters slept in the basements of churches like Wellington Avenue United Church of Christ, then assembled in Lincoln Park to coordinate their preparations for protests at the convention itself.

The city refused to grant permits for the festival or the convention protests that followed. This allowed police to use the law that Chicago parks are closed after 11 p.m. as an excuse to chase the protesters out with tear gas and billy clubs.

Over a thousand demonstrators fled the attacking police, running from Lincoln Park into the streets of the adjacent Old Town neighborhood. Tear gas wafted into nearby residences and such unlikely places as the Playboy Mansion, radicalizing such unlikely people as the hedonistic Hugh Hefner, who would later fund some anti-Daley local political organizations.

Down the street at the Earl of Old Town folk club, legendary Chicago folk singer, future pub owner, and folk school teacher Ed Holstein was finally getting his big break, an opening at "The Earl." Unfortunately for Ed, the convention and demonstrations left an audience of only ten people to see his show.

As the convention began, the number of protesters in Grant Park swelled to more than 5,000. They were a mixture of groups from across the U.S., including the Chicago 7, leaders of various peace groups, the Yippies, and civil rights groups, who would later be tried in federal court for leading the protests. However, this was not primarily a civil-rights protest; the demonstrators were mainly peace and counter-culture groups contesting cultural issues. Most were white youth, as blacks had long ago learned how repressive the Daley police could be when putting down protests. Some demonstrators were expressing disillusionment with uptight American culture in general. Others, like Scott and I, were concerned with issues of democracy, the imperial presidency, segregation, and the Vietnam War. At question for all of us was the clash between law and order and participatory democracy. Though I did not completely agree with some like the Yippie leader Abbie Hoffman's message and methods, I knew we were all fellow travelers.

On the second day, I joined hundreds of demonstrators in the five-mile march from Grant Park to the convention center. Singing and chanting slogans, we marched peacefully, without police interference, through both black and white neighborhoods. The police finally stopped us well short of the convention center itself, even though the convention would not reconvene until evening.

Meanwhile, the fight on the convention floor was an echo of the battle between the demonstrators and the police in the streets and the parks. As memorialized in the photograph, Mayor Daley famously shouted epithets as Connecticut Senator Ribicoff charged from the podium that the Chicago police were acting like the Gestapo in putting down the demonstrations. At one point, opposition delegates spontaneously began singing "The Battle Hymn of the Republic" to protest the adoption of the more conservative Democratic platform and the nomination of Hubert Humphrey. Their singing protest completely shut down the convention for more than half an hour.

Delegates inside the convention waving a banner mourning Bobby Kennedy while singing "The Battle Hymn of the Republic"

Both the "revolutionaries" demonstrating in Grant Park and those of us fighting within the political system wanted an alternative society based upon community, as opposed to rampant, greedy individualism. Mayor Richard J. Daley and the forces of law and order wanted a society based upon laws, responsibility, respect for authority, and the status quo. Both points of view had merit, but my contemporaries and I wanted change and we wanted it now. We were part of a worldwide clash of young and old, liberal and conservative, change vs. keeping things the way they were.

In the end, mere months after we had defeated incumbent President Lyndon Johnson in the primaries, the old guard, led by President Johnson and Mayor Daley, successfully nominated Hubert Humphrey over the opposition of the McCarthy, Kennedy, and McGovern delegates. Our fight for McCarthy's platform was lost. Humphrey then lost to Richard Nixon in the November general election when many of us who supported McCarthy and Kennedy refused, wisely or unwisely, to vote for him.

The defeat was bitter, but in retrospect I realize that we were wrong to think that we could bring about change by starting at the top, electing a new president, and working our way down to the local level. It was naïve to assume that we could change the country in just a few years. Fifty years later our work is not done, and it has not all gone well. We have won some battles, but we have had to live with many more partial victories. We may have ended segregation, but we have not ended discrimination. We ended the Vietnam War, but we still live in an unstable and dangerous world. We have even less participatory democracy now than we did in the 60s.

As Tom Hayden, one of the Chicago 7 and author of the 1962 *Port Huron Statement*, our generation's manifesto, later wrote, "Rarely, if ever, in American history has a generation begun with higher ideals and experienced greater trauma than those lived fully in the short time from 1960 to 1968."

The Richard J. Daley political machine was at the height of its power in 1968. At the heart of the machine was an economic transaction. Everyone who stayed within it got something.

To get contracts or a job at City Hall, you worked your precinct and contributed money to the Democratic Party. If you were Irish and you delivered to the party, you got top jobs and the power to distribute them to everyone else. If you were Italian, Chicago Transit Authority jobs were open to you. If you were Polish or black, or any other significant racial or ethnic group, there were certain benefits and patronage jobs available just to you. Labor unions got sweetheart labor contracts. Businessmen got city contracts with thievery written between the lines.[1]

Politics in the city had little to do with ideology, platform promises, or charismatic leadership. On Chicago's North Side, where the McCarthy campaign had been hard-fought, not a single independent candidate had been elected to public office since the Great Chicago Fire of 1871. By 1968, rule by the Chicago machine was absolute.

---

1   Len O'Connor, Clout: *Mayor Daley and His City* (Chicago: Regnery, 1975), 9.

Campaigning for Bernie Weisberg

9

CREATING INDEPENDENT
POLITICAL ORGANIZATIONS

*Sometimes reforms require new institutions,
not just new laws or new elected officials.*

CHICAGO IS THE epitome of American politics. We hide nothing here, not even our flaws. It was the perfect place to begin testing our belief in the power of participatory democracy. Our precinct organization experiment would last a decade and leave a permanent mark on Chicago politics.

Our rout at the Chicago Democratic Convention taught us a valuable lesson: it was fruitless to gear up for a single electoral campaign against a patronage machine whose entrenched precinct hirelings worked from election to election. We would continue to lose elections unless we founded our own permanent, year-round, precinct-based organization. We needed the ability to contest each election and lead issue campaigns in the intervals between elections.

We also learned that discussions among fellow liberals at cocktail parties and fundraising events were not at the heart of electoral politics. To win, we had to have a permanent organization of precinct volunteers scattered throughout our entire congressional

73

district. So, in November, 1968, soon after the election was over, a group of ten veterans of the failed McCarthy campaign gathered in Scott's and my living room to do exactly that.

As we sat in a circle of chairs in our small apartment over a garage that had once been a horse stable, we were convinced we had to act to change things. From the McCarthy campaign experience, which was all of our introduction into Chicago and national politics, we were convinced we could succeed. So we formed an organization and named it IPO, the Independent Precinct Organization.

We may have been idealistic, but we were also aggressive and proactive, out to upend Chicago politics and defeat the machine that had dominated our city for a century. As entrenched as the machine was, Chicago politics was ripe for a change. Issues like civil rights and the Vietnam War were influencing ordinary citizens. Mayor Daley's "hammer down" methods at the Chicago convention did not sit well with much of the public. Reporters and cameramen who had been beaten by the police were beginning to understand firsthand what machine rule and autocracy leads to. For the first time, the media was willing to criticize Daley directly. In public opinion polls taken immediately after the convention, 60 percent of the people still supported Mayor Daley and the police. But that meant that 40 percent were now opposed. It was our job to fan the flames of opposition, particularly along the liberal lakefront.

If we could translate poor public opinion into the defeat of machine candidates in elections, then laws and court decisions could begin to undercut the whole patronage system – the base of the machine's power. Because without control of the government by the machine bosses, there would be no favors to hand out.

We already had a large and loyal base of political activists. People on Chicago's North Side had given thousands of dollars and worked countless hours to attempt to elect McCarthy delegates, with hundreds of volunteers doing door-to-door precinct work for the first time. We discovered that the outrage many felt at Chicago police brutality could be translated into a new electoral movement. In some ways, this presaged the Tea Party and Bernie Sanders' "Our Revolution" in the 21st century.

Because we focused on local elections, we also attracted citizens who had not been involved in national politics. They cared about the kind of alderman that represented them at City Hall, or the state legislator that represented them in Springfield. And ours was not an exclusive club. Although most of our members were liberal Democrats, we supported good-government Republican candidates and cooperated with the local Republican Party on some reform proposals.

Of course, such an organization – particularly one out to change the world – has to have leadership. We were lucky that in the presidential campaign and the campaigns that followed we were able to recruit able leaders at all levels. I was chosen as Executive Director of IPO. Scott became our full-time office manager and was given a stipend to run the office we rented on Halsted Street, not far from our home. Our future neighbor Bob Houston and dozens of other friends and colleagues would provide leadership to the organization in its early days.

To become an IPO member, one had to pledge to give monthly financial contributions and to work on issue and election campaigns. Only those who made that commitment could vote to elect our officers and endorse the campaigns which we undertook. Every member was personally invested in our efforts – there were no mere spectators.

We were radically democratic. All of our decisions were made in an assembly of the membership after all the candidates appeared or the issue proposals were presented and debated. Our officers were elected for short 18-month terms, and almost none of us served for more than a few years in key positions. Any candidate or campaign we endorsed had to obtain a two-thirds vote of our membership present at the meeting. That served us well, because in future elections we would most often run our own Independent candidates for positions, not simply wait to endorse party candidates in general elections. And if we were to win these tough elections against the machine, we would have to be united.

Fr. Carl Lezak giving instructions at a Weisberg training session

This was, of course, in sharp contrast with the Democratic machine in which only the precinct captains, who were frequently government patronage workers receiving economic rewards, got into Party meetings, and all the key decisions were made by the bosses in closed door, backroom deals. And Democratic Party leaders not only held on to leadership posts for life, but through nepotism passed their powerful posts on to their sons – and later, their daughters.

In the fall of 1968, we banded our volunteers together and endorsed a slate of three Democrats and two Republicans running for offices in our district, from state legislator to congressman. Election results showed that we delivered more votes for these five candidates than they would have otherwise obtained. We did not endorse in the 1968 presidential campaign and many of us abstained from voting for Hubert Humphrey.

Our next campaign was to elect Bernie Weisberg as delegate to the Illinois Constitutional Convention, which would rewrite our outdated 1870 state constitution. We were up against two powerful Democratic Party machine candidates once again. But this time we would prevail.

The district was only two and a half wards in size, more manageable than the entire congressional district in which we had waged the McCarthy delegate campaign. And Bernie was an outstanding candidate who, in addition to his private practice, took on tough cases for the American Civil Liberties Union.

After distinguished service at the convention, which produced the best state constitution in the nation at the time, Weisberg was appointed a federal judge where he also served with distinction. His wife, Lois Weisberg, would go on to become the Commissioner of Fine Arts and Special Events for both Mayors Harold Washington and Richard M. Daley.

We immediately followed the Weisberg victory in 1969 by electing Bill Singer as alderman of the 44th Ward. Other victories, along with defeats, followed.

Bernie Weisberg, IPO candidate for 1969 Illinois State Constitutional Convention, giving his victory speech.

Our success, although gradual, was astonishing. Over time, we were able to elect more than two dozen "independent" or "reform" and "progressive" candidates, as we would now style them. We broke the machine's grip on Chicago's North Side and contributed to victories in larger elections such as that of Harold Washington as mayor in 1983 and 1987.

IPO couldn't last, however, under the conditions at the end of the 20th century – conditions which have only worsened today. In its decade of existence, IPO had depended on several hundred citizens willing to be volunteers and leaders for monthly meetings, community campaigns, and election campaigns every year or two. Unlike machine workers, who received financial rewards, we were rewarded only by electing candidates in whom we believed, meeting like-minded friends, and by the sense of having done our civic duty.

As times became tougher economically, and as women, who were often the backbone of the organization, got full-time jobs, fewer potential volunteers and leaders were available. We expected too much of them in an ever-more capitalistic society that made increasing demands in the workplace. For a time, we were able to save the organization and its participatory principles by merging it in 1979 with the Independent Voters of Illinois (IVI), a much older and established organization which had existed since World War II.

In its purer form, IPO lasted a decade and later had a democratizing effect on IVI, making it more participatory and precinct-work based. Reflections of our efforts appeared in Harold Washington's 1980s mayoral campaigns, the reform laws passed in his administration, and, to some degree, in Barack Obama's 2008 and 2012 campaigns for president. There is no direct line between our efforts and Obama's, because we played only minor roles in his campaigns. But his volunteers were powered by the same motivations and ideals as we were back in the 1960s and 1970s. Yet, in the end, our idealism failed under the pressures of pragmatism and changed economic conditions.

The experience of IPO would be repeated in the 44th Ward Assembly, an organization which also collapsed a decade after its founding. Here again, some of its essence remains in the current Participatory

Budgeting Project in some Chicago wards and in the neighborhood zoning hearings which some aldermen still hold.

It was discouraging to found idealistic organizations like IPO and, later, neighborhood government institutions, only to have them fail in time. But it was impossible for them to become permanent without government laws to support their existence, and in Chicago at that time the machine was dead-set against any form of participatory democracy.

Even though it failed, the fact that IPO lasted for a decade, or even that democratic civilizations exist at all, shows that better politics are possible. Although democracy lifts civilization by such idealistic efforts, it apparently does not become a permanent state of affairs. Democracies eventually fall, as did ancient Greece and the Roman Republic as it morphed into the Roman Empire.

Participatory democracy is not self-sustaining; it will always require effort. And although democracy often fails to endure, it always seems to be reborn when men and women are willing to make the sacrifices necessary to bring it back into being in the new forms required of new times.

Each time groups of citizens act for the common good rather than personal gain; each time they are empowered to decide for themselves what government should do rather than being told what government leaders purport to be doing for them; each time there is democratic deliberation, as there was in IPO, I am reaffirmed in my belief in "all power to the people."

In its early days, our IPO rode high on a string of successes.

In 1969, we elected Bernie Weisberg and Dawn Clark Netsch as delegates to the Illinois Constitutional Convention. Later the same year, we elected Bill Singer to City Council in the 44th Ward and narrowly missed electing John Stevens as 42nd Ward Alderman. In 1970, we elected Bruce Douglas and Jim Houlihan as state legislators and Dawn Netsch as state senator. We were on a roll.

But the Daley machine still held sway in Chicago and President Nixon was at the height of his power in Washington, D.C.

All the Independent Democratic officials we had elected were doing a good job, but they weren't instituting participatory politics in government itself. They weren't fulfilling our more radical agenda from the 1960s. It just wasn't enough.

Working the phones in my first aldermanic campaign, 1971

10

RUNNING FOR ALDERMAN

Sometimes you can fight city hall . . . and win.

IN THE WINTER of 1971, in snow and subzero weather, every workday morning found me standing at a bus or 'L' stop at 7 am, shaking hands with hundreds of bleary-eyed commuters as they caught transportation to their downtown jobs.

"Hi, I am Dick Simpson and I am running for 44th Ward alderman," I would say, thrusting a campaign brochure into their hands. Some stopped for a brief discussion of Chicago politics or campaign issues, most just hurried by to catch their ride downtown. But I met several thousand of my neighbors that way.

By the end of 1970, the success IPO was enjoying had become bittersweet. True, our liberal candidates were getting elected and representing us well. But to us true believers, something important was missing, something I really believed in: unswerving dedication to the principles of participatory democracy.

In addition, I was ready to move from the role of campaign manager to candidate, to run for office myself. So in 1970, on the strength of the election victories which IPO had won over the last two years, I laid plans to run for 43rd Ward alderman in the upcoming election of 1971.

Then came the decennial census of 1970. Chicago wards were redrawn, and Independent Democratic Alderman Bill Singer's home, along with half the ward he represented, was gerrymandered out of the old 44th Ward and into the 43rd Ward where Scott and I lived.

Bill was an Independent Democrat whose election IPO had supported two years earlier. If I were to run against him, it would not work politically – our group's votes would be split between the Independents and the Independent Democrats. This would play out two ways, neither of them good. First scenario: Bill and I would both lose. Second scenario: I wouldn't have enough of a base to overcome Bill, an incumbent who was doing a good job in the City Council, so he would win. It was easy to see that running against Bill, an ally and something of a friend, was not an option. It looked as if my run for City Council was dead in the water.

But as often happens with politics, things changed rapidly. Our citizen search committee, which was how IPO found and supported candidates in local elections, failed to find a suitable candidate to replace Bill Singer in the new 44th Ward. At their request, Scott and I met with a small group at Lois and Bernie Weisberg's home. Our friends Mark and Anna Perlberg were there, along with one or two others. We all knew each other from IPO and Bernie Weisberg's successful campaign for Constitutional Convention delegate, and they knew of my work in independent politics going back to the McCarthy campaign.

The group had already considered candidates like Fr. Carl Lezak, a Catholic priest. But for one reason or another, none of the other potential candidates had worked out or been willing to run. The 44th Ward Aldermanic Search Committee turned to me to be the Independent candidate in their ward.

There were major obstacles to my candidacy. It was late to be starting the campaign, and I lived in the wrong ward. When I have advised other candidates over the years, I always recommend they start their campaigns months earlier than I did. But sometimes opportunity knocks, and you have to take advantage of circumstances. It also helped

At a living room "coffee," with Mark Perlberg to my left

that with the redrawing of ward boundaries, there was no incumbent alderman. It is always easier to run for an open seat than to run against an entrenched incumbent.

Still, to make this work, we would have to move into the ward immediately. It would be Thanksgiving before we could launch the campaign, and Election Day was only three months, not years, away.

On the upside, we all had campaign experience, and the volunteer campaign leadership positions would be easy to fill. The half of the ward that Bill Singer had represented before the redistricting had been won by Independent candidates several times before. And the committee and my supporters knew I would be an energetic candidate.

A week after the informal meeting at the Weisberg's, and once the larger search committee formally endorsed me as the Independent IPO candidate, we began the process of moving from our coach house apartment on Freemont Street to a small apartment on Aldine just west of Broadway Avenue. Just after Thanksgiving, we quickly opened a centrally-located campaign office on Belmont, west of the 'L.'

The next challenge was to transform myself from campaign manager and political organizer to a good candidate, a difficult transition under the best of conditions. Those roles require very different skills: a switch from methodical organizer to spokesperson for the movement, from working behind the scenes to being up on stage. As a teacher and political organizer, I had experience with public speaking, so I didn't fear public speaking as some candidates do. But there was no guarantee that the transition would go well. Fortunately it did, and I benefited from both sets of skills throughout the rest of my political career.

I chose Marvin Jones, Scott's old boss from Bloomington, Indiana, as my first campaign manager because I could trust him and he was available to take the job. Unfortunately, he was not a good match, and before long I replaced him with a more experienced campaign manager from the Weisberg Constitutional Convention campaign. I was fortunate that Don Rose became the campaign's public relations guru and advisor, a role he would continue in for many of my campaigns. My campaign staff, along with many devoted volunteers who worked the precincts, made victory possible.

The campaign wasn't all politics. There was also a personal side to this election, and the other independent or reform campaigns we ran on the North Side of Chicago in those heady years. A number of women who had leadership roles in my aldermanic campaign ended up having their own careers, going on to more important positions. In some cases, it was going door-to-door as equals with their husbands that was empowering. The campaigns changed us all and bonded us together. As with many of the campaign workers in this and other campaigns, we would remain lifelong friends. In fact, reunions of some of these folks continue to occur now, fifty years later.

It was clear to us back then that this election was not going to be a cakewalk. The machine was alive and well, and looking to take back this aldermanic seat – especially since its chances of defeating Bill Singer in the new 43rd Ward were not good. And machine workers had learned some lessons from the recent defeats which we had given them.

Rather than running a tired old political hack like Ward Committeeman Eddie Barrett as they had done in Bill Singer's first aldermanic campaign, the machine put up a younger candidate this time around. He was James Kargman, a recent Northwestern University graduate

Being introduced by Studs Terkel at a fundraiser for my 1975 campaign

and computer software salesman. Stephen Yates, the son of the very popular 9th District Congressman Sidney Yates and himself a future judge, would be his campaign manager. The popular and moderate John Merlo, 44th Ward Committeeman and state senator, ran the Democratic Party political organization which orchestrated Kargman's campaign for the party. In short, these new faces for the machine were more appealing to the constituents in the ward. This wasn't your grandfather's old-fashioned Democratic Party political machine of even one or two elections back.

I brought my best game to the campaign, building it on a three-part platform. If elected, I promised that I would:

1. Open a full-time service office which would provide city services to everyone as a matter of right, and not as favors for voting for me.
2. Vote in City Council representing my Lakeview community and my conscience, not as a rubber stamp for the mayor and his political machine.
3. Create a neighborhood ward assembly (and neighborhood government) to direct my council vote and ward activities.

This platform distinguished me from my opponent, who was not free to make such "radical" promises in the era of party boss control. This positioned me as the Independent, good-government candidate, opposed to the Daley machine. To win an election you must do two things: 1) have a clear campaign theme or message, and 2) be able to deliver that message to persuade the voters to vote for you, especially when you are opposing a powerful political machine who can promise voters jobs, favors, and contracts in exchange for their vote.

Because of the "police riot" of the 1968 Democratic National Convention, in which the press, as well as the demonstrators, had been tear gassed and beaten, much of the media were no longer the lap dogs of Mayor Daley. So I was fortunate to receive positive press coverage and newspaper endorsements as a young reformer battling the evil Democratic machine. But press coverage alone wasn't enough to make me an effective candidate, and there were things I struggled with. For instance, my staff and volunteers were constantly on my case about not smiling enough in my public talks and appearances. But despite the fact that I was unable to change my serious, somewhat doleful mien much, voters became convinced that I was honest, sincere, and capable. They seemed willing to vote counter to Alderman Paddy Bauler's famous saying after Richard J. Daley's 1955 election, that "Chicago ain't ready for reform." By 1971, at least in the new 44th Ward, they were indeed ready.

Campaigns like my aldermanic and congressional campaigns are both exciting and grueling. Those who have not been candidates or campaign officials do not understand exactly how difficult they are on candidates and their families, just like those of us who have not seen combat in war do not understand soldiers' experiences. Certainly election night is heady, standing before cheering supporters to claim victory. But first the day-to-day campaign grind must be endured.

Here is my simultaneously exhilarating and exhausting campaign schedule for the typical day of Wednesday, February 3, 1971:

6:00 am   Get up and dressed for the day

7:30 am   Aldine and Sheridan bus stop: handshaking with constituents on their way to work

9:15 am   Nettlehorst School, 442 W. Aldine: meet with PTA president, discuss school and neighborhood issues (part of the community campaign to meet with community leaders)

10:30 am   Francis Parker High School in Lincoln Park neighborhood: give speech on the election at school assembly (even though they are too young to vote, the students will tell their parents)

1:00 pm   LeMoyne School, 851 W. Waveland: meet with principal to discuss issues and problems at his school

2:00 pm – 4:00 pm   Door-to-door walking tour with Fr. Lezak (a priest at St. Sebastian's Church with many parishioners in the ward) to seek votes in West Side precincts

6:30 pm   Pat Boundin's home: campaign coffee to recruit votes, volunteers, and money

8:45 pm   Bob and Kate Kestnbaum's home: campaign coffee

9:45 pm   Irv and Carol Ware's high-rise building party room: campaign coffee

10:30 pm   Campaign HQ: weekly steering committee meeting

Midnight: Back home and to bed

Each morning before dawn, no matter how cold the Chicago weather, I was out shaking hands with constituents at bus and 'L' stops on their way to work. Each afternoon I spent two hours going door-to-door with community leaders or precinct volunteers meeting voters and seeking their support. In between, I made fundraising calls to get the money the campaign needed. Extra events like press conferences varied the schedule slightly, and on Tuesdays and Thursdays I also taught my two courses at the University of Illinois at Chicago. Each evening when there weren't community organization meetings or campaign debates in front of community audiences, I visited between three and five "coffees" to meet voters, recruit campaign volunteers, and also raise the money we needed to run the campaign.

I survived these busy days because of a lesson I had learned as a campaign manager: do at least one important thing first thing in the morning, before you get on with the other demands of the day. Write a speech, draft a lecture for your course, put together a calendar for the campaign, or plan a key event first. Once the day gets rolling, you can only respond to demands, not undertake major creative efforts. So after the bus or 'L' stops in the morning, I would devote some time to taking a major step forward before I became overwhelmed by the other demands, phone calls, requests, and routine activities which would inevitably occupy the rest of my time.

There were other stressors to the campaign than schedule demands. Echoing the bombing of the civil rights planning session in Austin during my college years, my wife received death threats for me on our home phone while I was on the campaign trail. I was, after all, running against the Chicago machine with its deep ties and history with the Chicago mob.

My best guess remains that the threats came because I promised to curb the activities of the much-hated Lincoln Towing Company, which was known for frequently towing cars of ward residents, even from legal parking places. This was reported in the newspaper stories of the time and even made famous by folk singer Steve Goodman's popular song, "Lincoln Park Pirates," which satirized the company and its employees.[1] Having survived being ostracized at Texas A&M, the bombing of our civil rights meeting in Austin, and the threats yelled from cars driving by the stand-in demonstrations at the movie theaters, I simply ignored the threats. I was young enough to feel invincible, and

---

1   After I was elected, Steve actually did the research for the song in my aldermanic office.

refused to be deterred and forced to live my life in fear and conformity.

On Election Day, I visited all 64 precincts in the ward. I made sure that my precinct volunteers were in their places, contacting voters, getting them to the polls, and watching closely that the election was not stolen, which was a real possibility in Chicago at the time.

Hispanic leaders endorsing my campaign for alderman

By the afternoon, I went home for an hour or two, then headed back out to greet commuters on their way home from work, trying to get that last possible vote. Then there was nothing to do but wait at home with Scott for the phone call that would tell me whether I had won or lost, and the summons to the celebration or defeat at our campaign headquarters.

Finally the news came: I had won. By the time we arrived at our Belmont office, the results had been called in by our poll watchers in each precinct. I had won with 54 percent of the vote. By 10:30 pm, I had been elected as an Independent Alderman of the 44th Ward, made my victory speech, and was ready to fight City Hall.

Campaign workers and families surround me in this campaign brochure photograph

The City of Chicago is divided into 50 wards. Each ward is represented by an alderman who serves a four-year term on the City Council. The mayor of Chicago presides over the City Council; its secretary is the city clerk.

During the 1970s, Mayor Richard J. Daley maintained iron-fisted control over the City Council. It essentially served as his rubber stamp.

In 1971, we had a fairly solid opposition bloc of seven aldermen. On very rare occasions we could reach a high of 14 votes against the administration's most controversial proposals.

By 1977, the opposition bloc had shrunk to only three as Alderman Leon Despres retired from the 5th Ward and other allies were defeated when they ran for mayor.

The eight years from 1971-1979 were characterized by a series of battles over the future of Chicago and the nation, played out on the stage of the Chicago City Council chambers.

Campaign button for my 44th Ward Alderman reelection campaign, 1975

11

CITY COUNCIL WARS

*Sometimes the fruits of your labor can
take a while to ripen – and someone else
may do the harvesting.*

FIGHTING FOR REFORMS in Chicago City Council looked the same to me as fighting for civil rights in Austin and attacking the political machine in election battles. So only a few months after my election as alderman, I dove headlong into one of my most famous clashes.

On July 21, 1971, I rose in the City Council chambers to challenge the appointment of Tom Keane Jr. to the relatively obscure Zoning Board of Appeals. To me, it was an ugly mix of nepotism and conflict of interest. I thought it was wrong, so I asked a few questions. The room exploded.

Tom Keane, Jr. was the son of Mayor Richard J. Daley's floor leader, Alderman Tom Keane, Sr., who was himself the son of an alderman. Tom Keane, Jr. was also vice president of Arthur Rubloff and Company, the biggest real estate company in Chicago. If he were to be appointed to the Board of Appeals, Tom Jr.'s decisions would directly affect the value of his company's properties.

I hesitated before opposing this appointment because Tom Jr.'s father was such a powerful ally of Mayor Daley. As floor leader, Tom Sr. was head of the finance committee. He was also a powerful ward committeeman, perhaps the second- or third-most powerful Democrat in Illinois after Daley himself (this was a few years before Keane Sr. would be convicted of political corruption and be sent to federal prison). Since 90 percent of important legislation has to do with money, he had immense political control over city budgets, contracts, and nearly everything of significance that passed through council chambers. To oppose his son's appointment would be seen as a personal insult, possibly causing my future legislative proposals to be thwarted.

Nevertheless, on the council floor, I declared, "This appointment poses the problem of the faith of our citizenry in our city government. Why is it that members of the same family get appointments in several sections of government and only large firms seem to get representation on boards dealing with zoning and construction?" It was a very short speech.

Mayor Daley interrupted and demanded to know how anyone could question him. "[T]he idea that I made this appointment because a man's name was Keane and he was the son of a famous member of this council! I made this appointment because I have known Tommy Keane, the boy I appointed, since he's been a baby. . . . Should that boy be told . . . that he shouldn't hold office because his name is Keane?"[1]

Daley was particularly angry that I was challenging nepotism. Nor did he have much respect for my profession. He continued, now more loudly, "Where are we going with these kind of educators? You are doing this to the young people of our country! … And [Simpson] is not the only one. He's typical of the large number [of professors] in

---

1   The text was pieced together from quotations from Harry Golden Jr., "Daley Assails Colleges for 'Agitation and Hate'," *Chicago Sun-Times*, July 22, 1971, 1, 4 and Bill Boyarsky and Nancy Boyarsky, *Backroom Politics* (Los Angeles: J. P. Tarsher, 1974), 21-22. They took their quotations from an audiotape of Daley's speech recorded by radio station WMAQ.

universities polluting the minds of the young people.... [F]rankly, if you're a teacher, God help the students that are in your class, if this is what is being taught."[2]

Once the shouting stopped, and after a half-dozen speeches by sycophant aldermen praising the appointment and Daley's tirade, Tom Keane Jr.'s appointment was approved by an overwhelming 44-2 vote. Only my liberal colleague and friend, 43rd Ward Alderman Bill Singer, voted with me against the appointment.

One of the reasons that Daley was so adamant in his defense of the Keane appointment was that he favored his own sons with government contracts, although it wasn't known at the time. The mayor gave no-bid city insurance contracts to the firm of Heil and Heil, which employed one of his sons. And the local Cook County Circuit Court, whose judges Daley elected, gave an extraordinary number of profitable court receiverships to another Daley son. So in 1973, Mayor Daley and I had another head-to-head round. I introduced a council resolution ordering Daley to account as to "whether he has unlawfully used his influence as Mayor . . . [for his sons] to receive undue preference." It was defeated 35-7, which was at least five votes more on my side than I had gotten in opposing the Keane appointment.

A few days later, local newspapers reported that at a closed session of the Cook County Democratic Central Committee, Daley blurted out, "If a man can't put his arms around his sons, then what kind of world are we living in? I make no apologies. If I can't help my sons, [my critics] can kiss my ass."[3]

These clashes over nepotism were similar to other battles over patronage, waste, and bad government policies that continued throughout my eight years in the City Council. The real battle was not the individual City Council votes, which I nearly always lost. Rather,

---

2   Ibid.

3   Harry Golden, Jr., "The Mayor in Crisis: He Can Take the Heat," *Chicago Sun-Times*, March 4, 1973, 3.

it was an ideological battle over the future of Chicago. It was not over winning individual votes or a single ordinance, resolution, or budget amendment – these were just markers in the much larger chess match. My few aldermanic allies and I were not just speaking to other aldermen, because no matter how factual or eloquent our arguments, we persuaded almost none of the machine aldermen to join our dissent and vote with us. Only a few, like Alderman Seymour Simon, were politically free to do so. Instead, through the media, we "played to the gallery," the larger public, in the hopes of gradually changing the course of Chicago politics and government.

Specific reforms like equal pay for female and male janitors, cutting the unnecessary patronage employees such as bridge tenders, garbage truck workers, and clerks, or providing freedom of information for both aldermen and citizens – these didn't happen when other reformers or I first introduced them on the floor of the City Council. They occurred years or even decades later, at which point they were no longer Alderman Paul Douglas, Len Despres, or Dick Simpson ordinances. Rather, they magically reappeared as Richard J. Daley or his mayoral successors' ordinances. Whenever a budget crisis or scandal would break, the political machine bosses would take up and pass one of our long-dormant reform proposals that they had previously defeated. Mayor Daley and his machine may have made it their mission to never admit an error or provide recognition for opponents like me, but step by step we dismantled the old machine. We had to resign ourselves to the idea that we wouldn't get the credit due to us, that the time for our reform ideas had usually not yet arrived. But over time we did improve the city and its government.

Our debates were not always polite and gentlemanly. As Republican Alderman John Hoellen, my frequent ally in the council and Republican candidate for mayor in 1975 would say, "Mayor Daley always looked at [opposition] as a kind of cancer, and he struggled to eliminate all of his opposition, to stifle it. He brooked no quarter.... Daley as a politician is as smart as an alley rat. He is vindictive, knows nothing but raw power and the sharp fang, and he will use it wherever he can in order to obtain his goals."[4] These political battles between Mayor Daley and his fearsome machine and us were harsh and total.

I enjoyed the dramatic fights on the City Council floor. Sometimes, walking down the long halls into the council chambers, I would fantasize that I was an armored knight going into battle. I liked the front-page news and television media coverage I gained as a reformer battling the machine. I liked being party to the behind-the-scenes fights to choose the next mayor when Daley died. Those were the heady aspects of my aldermanic career, and they yielded the iconic images such as the photograph of me standing alone on the council floor with the sergeant-at-arms and a policeman unable to quell my dissent.

Less glamorous – and more draining – were the 2,000 individual and organization service complaints that my aldermanic office and I fielded each year. Solving some of these real problems – like mediating a landlord-tenant dispute, getting welfare or social security payments to someone who desperately needed them, or getting a zoning variance so an older relative or grandparent could continue to live in an attic or basement apartment at a family's home – that was rewarding. So was building a new park or playground for neighborhood kids. It felt good to solve these real problems.

Some requests were frivolous or impossible to resolve. I got a call one Sunday morning from a funeral home owner about a city trash basket which had been knocked over under the 'L' near his business. Trash and paper were scattered about, and he wanted someone to come out and pick it up. Rather un-politically-correctly, I told him to pick it up himself.

In 1975, despite the entire might of the Democratic machine against me, I was reelected to a second four-year term by a margin of victory similar to that of my first election.

---

4   Quoted in Milton Rakove, *We Don't Want Nobody, Nobody Sent*. (Bloomington: Indiana University Press, 1979), 299, 304.

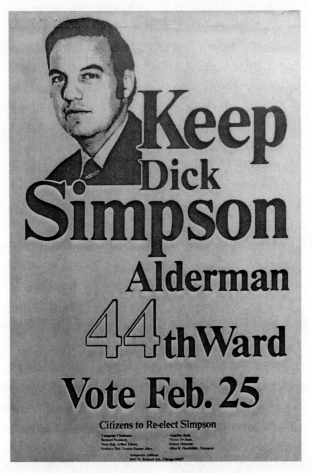

44th Ward reelection campaign poster, 1975

THROUGHOUT MY TIME as alderman, I worked over 80 hours a week. In the early years, I was still teaching full-time. By my second term, I reduced my university time by teaching one course a quarter instead of two. Despite that, it was still a long work week with two demanding jobs.

Taking a stressful phone call as 44th Ward Alderman, 1976

I did not run for alderman for the money. When I was first elected, the salary was only $8,000 a year. By the end of my second term it was raised to $17,000, but I did not keep even that meager salary. Alone among the aldermen in Chicago's history, I gave my aldermanic salary over to running our service office in the ward. Even with that, I still had to raise money with fundraisers and individual donations to fully fund the staff and office expenses.

At the end of my second term, I decided to end my aldermanic career. I did this for two reasons. First, as a practical matter, the 80-hour work weeks were difficult to maintain year after year. Second, and more idealistically, I wanted the neighborhood government institutions that I had founded to exist on their own, rather than because of the strength of my vision for them. This meant that the ward assembly, community zoning board, the Spanish-speaking assembly called *Asamblea Abierta*, and traffic review commission, in addition to IPO, had to continue on their own without support from the aldermanic office.

The units of neighborhood government did continue under my successor, Alderman Bruce Young, for two years after I retired. Bruce ended up resigning mid-term when he realized that there were some human problems even an alderman with ombudsman power and clout could not solve. He was a social worker, the former executive director of Jane Addams Hull House on Broadway. I believe that he became so frustrated with his inability to affect even the smallest changes, like preventing a tenant from being wrongly evicted, that he realized he had accomplished more at the head of his agency than he could as an alderman.

When Bruce resigned, the political machine recaptured the ward. First, the voters elected the popular ward committeeman and state senator, John Merlo, and then Democratic Party Ward Superintendent Bernie Hansen as 44th Ward Alderman. The machine was then free to destroy the neighborhood government we had built over the last decade. I hadn't been able to pass the laws necessary to make them permanent.

Two personal benefits came from my time as alderman, for which I remain grateful to this day. First, I earned a reputation for honesty, integrity, and standing up for my constituents which I would carry with me for the rest of my life. The modest fame and some notoriety I received because of my battles with City Hall allowed me to continue to get coverage in the media decades after I retired as alderman.

Second, I retained many friends from these years, as well as the McCarthy campaign and IPO period which preceded it. While some of these people have passed on, nearly fifty years later many of those friendships endure.

Part III

Love, Politics, Religion, Teaching

After the consciousness raising and civic activism of the 60s and 70s, many things were adrift sociologically in the United States in the 1980s. The divorce rate was at its peak – about half of all marriages ended in divorce throughout the entire decade.

Researchers and therapists may disagree on the cause for that spike, but one thing is on everyone's top-ten list of reasons for divorce: lack of communication.

Communication is key to holding a marriage together. When it breaks down, we don't feel connected to each other. Feeling like we are left on our own, we can suffer confusion, fear, and restlessness. And lack of conflict doesn't necessarily mean that all's well.

There are lots of reasons why communication dwindles in a marriage: if we become too wrapped up in ourselves; if we're so busy with external activities, even important ones, that we don't have the mental energy to listen to our partner; if we have never learned how to really listen and empathize with another person.

It takes self-awareness to judge what toll our focus on the outer affairs of our lives is taking on our relationship. The first, and maybe most difficult, step to being a better spouse is to know ourselves.

Scott, our dog Roger, and me, walking along Lake Michigan in happier days, 1971

12

WHEN COMPATIBILITY ISN'T ENOUGH

Love is a two-way street.
The less you travel it, the more it deteriorates.

WHEN SCOTT AND I married in 1964, we assumed that our commitment to changing the world and our love for each other would bind us together for a lifetime. We agreed to forego having children and entered the exciting new world of travel, education, and politics. Our life was interesting, to say the least: a year in Africa, the move to Chicago, working side-by-side in the McCarthy campaign, our work in IPO and the 44th Ward. I became an alderman, she became a professor at Rosary College, demanding that her students learn how to think and write with clarity.

Scott and I had always been compatible. We avoided the arguments that we watched harm other marriages. And we had fun together. We sometimes pretended that we had a dog named Roger. To Scott's surprise, one day I actually brought home a dog which we, of course, named Roger.

And so it seemed that our lives were good, and indeed making a difference in the world around us. But the demands of political campaigns, my university obligations, and my aldermanic career took an enormous amount of energy. Unlike our early years, when Scott was IPO's cofounder and office manager, she eventually became disengaged from the day-to-day work of politics and government and focused on her own career. Our lives and interests drifted apart. We found that the ties that bound our marriage had begun to unravel. We wondered if our decision to not have children might have been a mistake. It certainly made it easier for us to grow apart and go our separate ways.

For a while we continued doing the normal things that married couples do: visiting relatives; vacationing in Door County, Wisconsin; going to the symphony; spending time with friends. In the spring of 1979, just after I retired as alderman, we even took a wonderful two-week vacation to Greece and Italy, our first trip abroad since our African journey. It was a great shared experience; unbeknownst to us, it was also our last. For compatibility was not enough to hold our marriage together.

With the benefit of hindsight, I see that I exhibited a pattern which helped set us up for failure. As is true of many politicians, I desperately needed to feel loved. That is why we, as a type, seek applause and affirmation through elections, media attention, and public deeds. I threw myself into the early stages of our romance, but once my internal need for love was satisfied, I switched emphasis and focused on external activities – like African research, teaching, campaigns, and my aldermanic career.

As my job and political worries exhausted me, I became less emotionally available to Scott. Even when we were physically together, my mind and energies were always elsewhere.

This pattern made me oblivious to the fact that Scott was becoming unhappy in our marriage. Only later did she tell me that she was feeling stuck, that there was no room in our marriage for her to grow and change and move forward with her life. But at the time, I did not realize just how unhappy she had become.

Scott asked for a trial separation. Because she was so despondent, I felt that I had no alternative but to grant her request. But I held out hope that we would get back together, that this was merely a temporary setback. That with a little help, we would recover.

Still, our separation crushed me. I loved Scott, even if I didn't understand how to care for her emotional needs. Her rejection reinforced my own general sense of being unlovable. I did not know how to deal with my intense emotional pain. Now, for the first time in my life, I considered suicide.

A door of grace opened when Bill Mahin, a friend from the university with whom I had made several documentary films, invited me to move in with him. Newly divorced, Bill had a two-bedroom apartment near UIC on the historic block just east of Ashland Avenue on West Jackson Boulevard. We shared the rent and most evening meals, drinking wine and talking late into the night to help abate the pain and loneliness after divorce.

Even with Bill's friendship, I had no sense of purpose. My time as an alderman was over; surely my political career had ended. I had no political science projects to research, no books to write. Life looked bleak and pointless. It took effort just to keep moving, teaching my classes by day and coming home to Bill's apartment every night.

But somehow, being around Bill's young children when they visited on the weekends made me realize that life was still worth living. Bill and I started exercising, running laps after school a number of days a week. It took about six months, but I gradually began to recover my sense of self and purpose.

Talking with Bill about my divorce helped relieve the pain and pressure, but it wasn't a magic cure. I also saw a therapist and experienced what is known as intervention therapy. He helped me begin to remember my dreams and understand how some of my childhood experiences had shaped me, for better or worse, and were still affecting my outlook and life choices.

The first dream that came to me was a hieroglyph, or single image. It was the sarcophagus of a young girl, like one I had seen in Scott's and my trip to Siena, Italy. On one level, it was the image of the baby sister I never saw because she was stillborn when I was three years old. My therapist and I used this image to explore the years when my father was away at war and Mother was very sad, having lost her baby and wondering if she would lose her husband, as well. As an only child, that may have been when I learned to be a "good boy" and not disturb Mother in her grieving.

At another level, the sarcophagus dream represented the death of my nurturing side that had no space to develop in the "macho" Texas of my youth or my adult political activities. The divorce made room for personal growth, but it was forced upon me at a price I would not have chosen to pay.

For the first six months after our separation, I held on to the hope that Scott and I would get back together. But not long after our separation she fell in love with a man who had been a former student, who she eventually married. She moved on. I had to accept my new reality. In 1980, after sixteen years of marriage, we filed for a consensual divorce and stood together in the courtroom when it was granted.[1]

A quote from author Anne Lamott captures my feeling about the divorce best:

> *You will lose someone you can't live without, and your heart will be badly broken, and the bad news is that you never completely get over the loss of your beloved. But this is also the good news. They live forever in your broken heart that doesn't seal back up. And you come through. It's like having a broken leg that never heals perfectly – that still hurts when the weather gets cold, but you learn to dance with the limp.*

---

1   Ironically, our case was heard by Judge Edward Marsalek, whom I had defeated in my aldermanic reelection campaign and whose wife had served in my 44th Ward assembly.

Losing Scott was the biggest emotional blow of my life. I would go on to suffer many other losses, but none as great as this. After a decade, I would be able to meet her for a friendly cup of coffee and reminiscence from time to time. But the wounds of our divorce would never entirely heal. I learned to dance with the limp.

When President Nixon was forced to resign after the Watergate break-in and cover-up, the Democrats made great gains. Although Republican Vice-President Gerald Ford became president, the post-Watergate elections of 1974 brought in a wave of new activist, liberal Democrats to Congress.

In 1976, Democratic Governor Jimmy Carter was elected president. He is generally accounted to have been ineffective because of hands-on micromanaging and foreign policy failures, including the Iran hostage crisis. But Carter did continue the social justice programs of the Democrats. By the end of his term, he was looking to strengthen initiatives like neighborhood government programs.

However, in 1980, Carter was defeated by Ronald Reagan, who ushered in the Republican conservative revolution. Democratic members of Congress originally cooperated with the tax cuts and trickle-down economic theory of Reaganomics. But as it became ever clearer that Reagan's increased defense expenditures and cuts in social programs would destroy the social safety net, public opinion began to shift. It took a few years, but by the 1984-1985 budget, Congress began to put the brakes on further cuts to social spending.

44th Ward Assembly, 1977

13

IMPERMANENT INSTITUTIONS

If we're unaware of destructive cycles,
we're bound to repeat them.

MY POLITICAL LIFE and married life had collapsed. Now the political institutions which I had founded began to fall apart.

The first to falter was the Independent Precinct Organization. After a decade of existence, and with the changing social and economic conditions, there simply weren't enough people willing to carry the load. To save itself from extinction, the group merged with the Independent Voters of Illinois. As IVI-IPO, it changed and adapted, but became less a beacon of participatory politics and more a general reform organization.

Next to fall were the neighborhood government institutions I had founded in the 44th Ward. When my successor, Alderman Bruce Young, resigned halfway into his term, it was as if the air got let out of the balloon. The Democratic machine replaced Bruce with John Merlo first, then Bernie Hansen. Both men simply closed the doors to the 44th Ward Assembly, Community Zoning Board, *Asamblea Abierta*, and the Traffic Review Commission. Merlo and Hansen allowed long-existing neighborhood organizations like the Lake

View Citizens Council to continue, but the machine installed some of its precinct captains as leaders.

This type of pendulum swing in politics and government is common – a strong leader takes bold steps forward, then he or she is followed by a leader who consolidates those gains, only to have a more conservative leader swing policies and programs back the other way. For example, John F. Kennedy was followed by Lyndon Johnson, then by Nixon and Reagan. On a smaller scale, I was followed by Alderman Bruce Young who continued my policies initially, only to have them reversed by the Democratic Party regulars.

The National Association of Neighborhoods (NAN), of which my 44th Ward neighborhood government institutions had been a part, and in which I had been a national officer, was another reversal. By 1980 it was on the verge of financial collapse. I supported the black political leaders who took it over, but they were less able to retain the white neighborhood organizations and their leaders as part of the group. When federal grants ran out and a number of dues-paying groups withdrew, funding dried up. This schism came at the same time that the Carter administration, which had been favorable to neighborhood government, was replaced by the Reagan administration, which was not.

The Chicago reform movement was also sputtering. Mayor Harold Washington rejuvenated it when he was elected in 1983. When he died suddenly in 1987, his successor, Mayor Eugene Sawyer, carried out a number of Washington's reform proposals and policies as he had no programs of his own. But Washington's was the last progressive mayoral administration in Chicago. From then on, reform mostly waned as a new machine under Richard M. Daley took over.

Beyond the political, other doors were closing to me as well. Casting about for ways to get my life moving forward, I tried to pick up the thread of African political research that I had begun in 1966. Perhaps if I could return to Sierra Leone, Liberia, and Nigeria to see for myself their failed experiments in democracy over the two decades of my absence, I would be able to complete my book, *Reinventing Democracy*, which

I had started years earlier. For two years, I tried and failed to receive grants to return to Africa.

Since overseas study was not to be, I sought to become department head at UIC. To my great frustration, while the political science department voted to make me chair, it was vetoed by the university administration. I applied to other universities and liberal arts colleges to chair political science departments or become college president. Not a single interview ensued. Discouraged, I concluded that I had become too controversial for a university administrative position.

Next, I applied to become executive director of the Wieboldt Foundation. It seemed like a natural fit, since I had worked with community organizations in Chicago for two decades and was by now a nationally-recognized expert in neighborhood empowerment. But I lost the position to another candidate.

And so, despite my best efforts to the contrary, the life I had built for myself in Chicago seemed to have crumbled. Yet, as often happens, out of the rubble I discovered an opportunity to rebuild.

As soon as I began to heal emotionally, I became politically active again. This time I stepped into the roles of organizer and protest leader instead of campaign official and alderman.

In September, 1981, I joined over 250,000 people in a demonstration against Reaganomics in Washington, D.C. While I was there, I tried, unsuccessfully, to get funding from foundations and labor unions for our efforts back in Illinois. I failed and was also disappointed when no permanent institutions or organizations grew out of this massive rally. It was a pattern of protest, however, that was destined to be repeated with the inauguration of President Donald Trump some 35 years later. Likely the pattern of resistance will be repeated as well.

As it became ever clearer that Reagan's proposed increased defense expenditures and draconian cuts in social programs were destroying the social safety net, Chicago organizations being harmed by Reaganomics formed a coalition named the Illinois Coalition Against Reagan Economics (ICARE). Because of my previous visibility as alderman, I was chosen as co-chairman and spokesman for this group comprised of agencies like the National Association of Social Workers, IVI-IPO, and various civil rights organizations.

In May, 1982, when President Reagan's helicopter touched down at Meigs Field, I was leading a demonstration of 5,000 Chicagoans carrying signs opposed to Reaganomics. Our arguments against the Reagan budget were compelling and tied into powerful emotions. Yet our efforts were like trying to empty the ocean with a spoon, as conservative forces still controlled the national government.

Meanwhile, in Washington, congressman and future Chicago Mayor Harold Washington was leading the fight against Reagan's policies which were particularly harmful to his black South Side constituents. But he was not yet able to rally the necessary votes to defeat most of the budget cuts to social programs. The more pragmatic and powerful Democratic congressmen like Dan Rostenkowski, head of the powerful Ways and Means Committee, supported Reagan and made deals with the new Republican administration. Yet, the pendulum would eventually swing back our way. In the end, we would prevail, elect more liberal presidents like Bill Clinton and Barack Obama, and reestablish social programs.

IN AN UNEXPECTED note of grace, one of the first steps along my path to healing came in the form of a woman named Beatrice Briggs.

I had met Bea in passing during my second aldermanic campaign, for which she had given a coffee to recruit volunteers. When I became single, a mutual friend reintroduced us.

Bea owned her own public relations firm and was the executive director of the Chicago String Ensemble. She was drawn to many of the same things I was craving, and encouraged me to renew my interest in spirituality and explore yoga and meditation for the first time.

I hadn't known what to expect in a new relationship after my separation from Scott, and perhaps I should have been a bit more wary and thought more about the long term. But by August, 1984, we were engaged. By February, 1985, we were married. Unfortunately, our marriage was brief, lasting only two years.

Bea's daughters now became my step-daughters. The wise 16-year-old let me know early on that she wouldn't get emotionally involved until I had been around a few years. But her younger sister and I bonded well from the start. It took some adjustment on my part because I had no children of my own, but my stepdaughters taught me to play, to nurture, and to see the world

Bea Briggs, 1982

differently. With Scott, I had made the choice not to have children. But as with the role in my healing that Bill Mahin's children had played, having step-children was a great blessing.

I savored the freedom my new life gave me to explore the inner, spiritual aspects that had gone undeveloped in my external-oriented life of politics and teaching. I joined Bea in becoming a vegetarian, and we explored yoga and meditation together. During our time together, I tried various techniques of self-discovery, from psychotherapy and the Progoff Life Context Journal techniques to past-life regressions.

Bea helped me to renew my spiritual journey. I reconnected with my younger self, the youth who had preached sermons as a Boy Scout and was active in Methodist youth work at A&M and University of Texas. I returned to religion, but now it included Eastern religious and spiritual practices.

About this time, Bea began taking M.A. classes with the controversial Catholic priest Matthew Fox, at the Institute in Culture and

Creation Spirituality (ICCS) at Mundelein College. Through Matt and his institute, I met the theologian and philosopher Thomas Berry. We created an ad hoc group of religious, political, and community leaders to support the adoption of the World Charter for Nature at the United Nations, which Berry was helping to shape in this very early stage of the environmental movement. I also met John Giannini, who became my Jungian therapist and, later, lifelong friend until his death in 2017. Theologian Matthew Fox and I team-taught a course on politics and religion at the Institute as well.

At first, Bea and I enjoyed a bond of love and mutual support as she worked on her M.A. at ICCS, and I did my university, political, ecumenical, and church work. But the long, hard hours spent on these efforts took me away from my new family as many as three nights a week. My image of myself as advocate, a rock in the river of time and buffer against the decay which cascaded around me, caused me to struggle to find balance between political over-commitment in the external world and new spiritual growth in my interior world.

By early 1986, my relationship with Bea was strained. Bea's graduate school studies were draining her energy, and I was not open and emotionally present. I feared that our marriage would not last. But we worked at it, and by spring, hope prevailed. I thought I would be able to have it all: love, a spiritual life, a new political role, and teaching. In my journal, I noted: "Spring has come after a long winter."

Then, out of the blue, I experienced a vision that would alter the course of my life. Sitting at my sister-in-law's wedding, I vividly saw myself in the place of the Episcopal priest conducting the ceremony. Like an indelible snapshot, the image stayed with me. There was no sense of foreboding or peril if I ignored it, but I was compelled to decipher its meaning.

My family has a tradition of preachers. On Mother's side, Grandfather Oscar Felts had been a Nazarene preacher, as were my two of my uncles. My father's lineage went back to four ministers at the time of the American Revolution. If this turned out to be a calling into the ministry, my unique combination of teaching, politics, and activism in the work of the Lord would look very different from theirs. Nevertheless, it was in my blood. After some initial resistance and much meditation and reflection, I concluded that the vision was a legitimate call to a religious vocation. The United Church of Christ ministers and congregation at Wellington Avenue UCC, the church family I had joined when I married Bea, confirmed my call. At forty-two years of age, I was to go to seminary and become an ordained minister.

I may have been called to the ministry, but I still had life lessons to learn. Despite my new beginning and the happy days which followed, I once again let myself get cut off from my feelings and sharing emotions. I had forgotten that physical closeness comes from emotional closeness. In all the busyness of life, Bea and I had lost our connection. Late in 1986, she asked for a separation, and I did not contest the divorce which followed. Our connection with each other remained positive but distant after we were no longer a couple. But once more, I found myself alone.

Chicago's Red Squad was created in the early 20th century to spy on anarchists and labor organizers. By the 1960s, it was being used extensively by the Chicago police to target anyone who opposed Mayor Daley or official government policies like the disastrous War in Vietnam or racial segregation.

The federal government's principal domestic spying program was called COINTELPRO (Counterintelligence Program). The FBI, assisted by military intelligence agencies and cooperating local police departments, first set its sights on the Communist Party. The intelligence mission was later expanded to include civil rights activists, anti-Vietnam organizers, feminist movements, and anyone government agencies deemed to be opposed to the political status quo.

COINTELPRO methods included harassment, exposure, and prosecution for political crimes. Sometimes their methods worked; sometimes they backfired. If necessary, the FBI resorted to fraud and illicit actions.

Both COINTELPRO and the Chicago Red Squad compiled dossiers on whoever dared to oppose Boss Daley or Presidents Johnson or Nixon. They did so by direct surveillance, wiretaps, attending meetings and classes, "black bag" office break-ins, and by photographing demonstrations to identify opponents. They also infiltrated organizations with agent provocateurs who disrupted meetings, urged violent actions so that activists would get arrested, and generally undermined local efforts to organize for political change.

In the 1960s and 1970s, protests like this were photographed and carefully watched by the Chicago Red Squad, the FBI, and even U.S. Army spies

14

POLICE SPYING AND
REFORM BY LAWSUIT

*Sometimes the courts can bring more reform
than protests or elections.*

IN 1968, A military intelligence officer out of Evanston, Illinois, was assigned to spy on my classes at the University of Illinois at Chicago. He scribbled notes from my lectures and the readings I assigned.

From his reports, I later learned that books like *The Communist Manifesto* and *The Port Huron Statement* by the radical Students for a Democratic Society made a strong impression on him, while he ignored the fact that I taught the Declaration of Independence and the conservative philosophy of Edmund Burke in the same classes. The officer concluded that I was a leftist-pinko-communist sympathizer, who as Mayor Richard J. Daley put it, was "polluting the minds of young people." Of course, my political views were hardly secret, as I was a political organizer and soon to be an elected alderman. Nevertheless, someone thought it necessary to have an intelligence officer monitor my classes for several years.

In 1974, while I was an alderman, I met with a number of like-minded community leaders and political activists in a dank church basement on Chicago's West Side. Exercising our democratic right to free and vigorously-contested elections, we were seeking to build a coalition to run a slate of candidates for county offices against Daley machine candidates. As we later discovered, our effort failed in part because a police spy from the notorious Red Squad had infiltrated our group to undermine our coalition. As a result, we were unable to run opposition candidates for county offices in the 1974 local elections.

All this spying by the police and federal government had a chilling effect on our political mobilization efforts. People became afraid to join dissident organizations, to speak out against the government, or to join in protests for fear that a dossier would be created on them. Mayor Daley went so far as to order the Red Squad to spy on his political enemies and to report to him the information they collected. Even leaders of Daley opposition groups came to distrust each other, fearing that some activists might be police informants or spies.

By 1975, we had had enough. I joined with two dozen other individuals and organizations in filing the *ACLU v. City of Chicago* lawsuit. Citing our First Amendment rights, we sued to end the Chicago Police Department's infiltration and spying activities. The plaintiff list included elected officials like Alderman Leon Despres, U.S. Senator Adlai Stevenson III, and myself, and community and political organizations like the ACLU, Operation PUSH, Independent Voters of Illinois, and American Friends Service Committee. All of us had been spied upon while doing legal, non-criminal activities. Our only sin was opposing Mayor Daley and President Nixon.

Most lawsuits are unbearably dull; Party A sues Party B, maybe someone wins some money. On the other hand, some lawsuits, like *Brown v. Board of Education of Topeka*, can have momentous effect. *ACLU v. City of Chicago*, later nicknamed the "Spy Suit," was such a case.

In this lawsuit, we and our attorneys proved that City of Chicago officials "directly authorized or ratified unlawful government intrusions."[1] Their agents covertly infiltrated, participated in, and observed plaintiffs and thousands of others in our lawful political activities. They stole organization membership lists and private information, including what was said in private. They photographed and taped us as they sought "to actively disrupt or misdirect [our] activities." [2]

Police Red Squad Agent Porter was a prime example. He infiltrated Operation PUSH, a civil rights organization led by Rev. Jesse Jackson, rising to become head of their Men's Division. Other organizations like American Friends Service Organization (a Quaker group) and the Independent Voters of Illinois (a political organization opposed to Mayor Daley's machine politics) were the victims of "black bag" jobs in which their offices were broken into and ransacked, and wiretaps were planted to monitor their activities. As part of the evidence in the ACLU case, the FBI admitted to at least 500 warrantless office break-ins in Chicago alone. Far from being isolated incidents, these were the norm of the time.

ACLU v. City of Chicago was finally settled in 1982. As part of the settlement, we were awarded $325,000 in damages. Each plaintiff organization received $25,000, and each individual received $10,000. I helped organize the individual plaintiffs to contribute $1,000 each to a fund set up at the Crossroads Foundation to support First Amendment Rights cases and organizing in the future. $13,000 of the money received by individual plaintiffs and nearly all the money received by the organizations was used to continue the fight for Constitutional and human rights.

The court settlement caused the Red Squad to be disbanded, a consequence much more important than the monetary award. At least in Chicago, it also curtailed the FBI's "political spying, intrusion

---

1   ACLU et. al. v. City of Chicago et. al. reprinted in "Police Spying: ACLU v. City of Chicago" in Chicago's Future in a Time of Change, ed. Dick Simpson (Champaign, Il: Stipes, 1993),155.

2   Ibid., 156.

and disruption."[3] It ended unwarranted wiretapping and electronic surveillance back in the days before the Internet. For another 27 years, the consent decree would be monitored and enforced, until a federal district court agreed to dissolve it in 2009. Unfortunately, after the terrorist attacks of September 11, 2001, the National Security Administration instituted even broader spying on American citizens, allowing for monitoring of telephone and Internet communications. But for decades, our lawsuit promoted First Amendment rights and freedoms.

AS WE LEARNED from *ACLU v. City of Chicago*, reforms can be brought about by lawsuit as well as elections. To that end, I have been involved in a half dozen major lawsuits either as a direct witness of corrupt acts, a plaintiff, or an expert witness.

In 1974, I testified in Alderman Tom Keane's federal prosecution for corruption, for which he was found guilty and sent to jail – the same Tom Keane who was the long-time head of the City Council's finance committee and whose son's appointment to the Zoning Board I opposed back in 1971. Keane Sr. was also a Chicago lawyer. When his clients wanted to use his "clout" to obtain zoning variances, tax reductions, etc., they would pay him "legal fees." Through both of my terms as alderman I attended every single finance committee meeting, even though I wasn't actually a member of the committee until my second term in office after 1975. Since I had witnessed each vote, I was able to testify that when these "deals" were approved by the finance committee, the fact that Keane was making a back-room profit from the companies that were getting favorable treatment was never disclosed. Had I known about the bribes, I never would have voted for the variances.

Between 1969 and 1983, I was called as an expert witness in a number of the famous *Shakman* lawsuits. In them, Michael Shakman challenged the city's patronage hiring system. The outcome of these lawsuits eventually made patronage hiring illegal and allowed former

---

3   Ibid., 162.

employees who were fired for political reasons to sue to get their jobs back, along with payments of damages for their illegal firing.

Of all the reform lawsuits, the *Shakman* decrees were probably the most consequential in changing Chicago politics and government. They sharply curtailed political patronage, which was the backbone of the Chicago political machine. Advising Mayor Harold Washington as his transition team co-chair, I argued for his signing the consent decree which settled the cases with the City of Chicago, which he did. Even with the *Shakman* cases settled, it would take many years and many more lawsuits to effect that monumental political change.

We also used lawsuits to curtail the practice of gerrymandering. The City of Chicago was required to redistrict its wards with every decennial census. In most decades, it gerrymandered the new ward maps for both political benefit and to limit the number of minority aldermen in the City Council.

When lawsuits were filed to stop this, I was called as an expert witness. I produced studies proving that the racial composition of the City Council made a difference to its voting and policy decisions. This was stating the obvious, as it was pretty well understood by everyone who paid attention. However, the City of Chicago's corporation counsel fought me tooth and nail in deposition to discredit my testimony. The corporation counsel team subpoenaed my files, interviewed colleagues, and disrupted my professional life. They commissioned studies by other political scientists from other parts of the country to try and cast doubt on my statistical findings. They went so far as to call the editor of the *Journal of Urban Affairs,* who had published one of my studies of the Chicago City Council, to get the private peer review critiques the journal used in deciding whether to publish my article. The editor, Dennis Judd, who I didn't know at the time, refused to release the peer reviews.[4] In the end, my evidence was admitted as part of the case.

---

4   I would later recruit Dennis to come to UIC where he and his wife, Nan, became among my closest friends.

As a result, wards had to be redrawn and new elections held. These court-ordered redistrictings resulted in more minorities being elected, including the critical 1986 redistricting which gave Harold Washington the council majority by which he could govern and pass pent-up reform legislation his council opponents had blocked.

Another example was a case brought against a suburban library board to stop them from spending their funds illegally. Called as an expert witness, I testified that government funds cannot be used to influence the way citizens vote on issues like bond referendums. Even though I supported the bond issue to improve the library, I testified against this wrong use of public funds.

In all of these cases, we were seeking reforms by court or administrative decisions that we were unable to win by way of elections. From my perspective as a witness, expert witness, and consultant, these court battles were just as contentious, hard fought, disruptive, time consuming, and bitter as my more public City Council floor fights or election battles. But since we often prevailed in the legal arena, it was a successful strategy and worth the effort. It was political war by other means.

Over 300 American jurisdictions have become "sanctuary cities," limiting their cooperation with the federal government in enforcing immigration law. Within these safe zones, people who are in the country illegally need not fear that police will cooperate in deporting them or breaking up their families. If they are in jail for breaking local laws, they will not be turned over to immigration authorities upon release. In theory, these immigrants are therefore more willing to use health and social services, enroll their children in public schools, and report crimes.

Chicago has a long history of providing sanctuary to those who need it. In the late 1800s, the Chicago Common Council directed the police force to refuse to assist in apprehending and removing slaves. It found that the Fugitive Slave Act of 1850 "undermined justice and dishonored humanity."[1]

In 1985, Mayor Harold Washington declared Chicago to be a sanctuary city with Executive Order 85-1: "all residents of the City of Chicago, regardless of nationality or citizenship, shall have fair and equal access to municipal benefits, opportunities and services.... No agent or agency shall request information about or otherwise investigate or assist in the investigation of the citizenship or residency status of any person..." His order has been renewed by all Chicago mayors since. As Mayor Washington stated, "We will not be party to infractions of [people's] civil rights."

---

1   Wellington Avenue Church member Craig B. Mousin, "A Clear View from the Prairie: Harold Washington and the People of Illinois Respond to Federal Encroachment of Human Rights," *Southern Illinois University Law Journal* 29, (Fall 2004/Winter, 2005): 285-295, https://ssrn.com/abstract=2997657.

Newsgroup Chicago, Inc., 1984/photo by Al Podgorski

Declaring the Wellington Avenue UCC Nuclear Free Zone in 1984

WELLINGTON: A CHURCH OF ITS TIME

What seems like loss can actually be progress.

"OUR FATHER/MOTHER WHO are in heaven...." Thus begins the Lord's Prayer as recited by the activist congregation of Chicago's Wellington Avenue Church.

On July 1, 1984, in a service attended by friends, supporters, and my mother, I was ordained as a Minister of Urban Mission at Wellington Avenue United Church of Christ. I was given the authority to preach God's word, administer the sacraments, and exercise the responsibilities of teacher and pastor. My vocation was to attempt to reconcile politics and religion in a mission of social justice.

I served as Minister of Urban Mission to this United Church of Christ congregation for two decades. During that time, I participated in its transformation from run-of-the-mill church to an activist congregation. This transformation came about as we asked ourselves, "What does the Word of God as recorded in the Hebrew and Christian scriptures have to say to the people of Wellington and to our community this day? What does it mean to live faithfully in the midst of the challenges of the 20th and 21st centuries?"

The changes these questions prompted were dramatic, for we became part of the social and political struggles of our time.

With my mother at my Wellington ordination ceremony, July, 1984

In its first transformation, Wellington became congregation-run, rather than a clergy-dominated congregation. The laity determined the church budget, hired the pastor, and controlled most church decisions. This was in our DNA, as it were, because we came from a Congregationalist tradition. But we took it further than many other Protestant churches, giving the lay people full partnership in planning and conducting worship services.

Once the laity was empowered, the second transformation was to give women equal power as liturgists, members of the governing church council, and presidents of the congregation. Wellington also ordained women very early, well before most other denominations and faiths.

As early as the 1970s, we began using inclusive language in the Lord's Prayer and in scripture readings, giving clear recognition that women are equal with men. We had gays and lesbians as lay leaders in the congregation as well and performed same-sex marriages long before it was allowed by law.

The third transformation at Wellington changed how it used its property, from a church building used only by the congregation on Sundays to a home for many movements, social services, and causes every day and night of the year. Our basement became, in turns, a shelter for the homeless, a daycare center, and a center for homeless youth.

The second floor was transformed into a professional theater space, housing the acclaimed Timeline Theater. Community organizations, political meetings, and self-help groups like Alcoholics Anonymous now used the sanctuary and meeting rooms.

The fourth transformation was political. Even before the Civil War, our denomination had been filled with abolitionists. We continued that tradition of radical politics by housing protestors at the 1968 Democratic National Convention, welcoming African-Americans and Latinos as members, and including leaders from the anti-apartheid movement in South Africa, as well as undocumented refugees from Central America. On a symbolic level, Wellington joined the movement to eliminate nuclear weapon arsenals in all countries of the world and became a Nuclear Weapons Free Zone in 1984.

The members at Wellington also became politically active. Before I even joined the congregation, they had supported my campaigns for alderman and my two runs for Congress. Together we worked hard for the election of Harold Washington in 1983 and 1987, and for progressive candidates in the following years. Members of the congregation enthusiastically supported the presidential campaigns of Barack Obama in 2008 and 2012, and Hillary Clinton in 2016.

One of our boldest political acts was to become a sanctuary church, the first one in the North (one had earlier been created at a church in New Mexico). The first Guatemalan refugees that we housed were Ariel Muralles and his sister-in-law, Maria Paz. Ariel and his brother had both been teachers and political activists in Guatemala. His brother "disappeared," killed by death squads, although he was never charged with a crime. When Ariel and Maria were threatened, they fled through Mexico and Arizona and were brought by religious leaders to Chicago for sanctuary in our Wellington church building.

With the assistance of six North Side Chicago churches which helped to provide food and funding, we housed them in a small apartment in the church for two years. Whenever they spoke publicly about the terror in their home countries, they wore scarves

© Noel Neuburger

Guatemalan refugees with Rev. David Cheverie, Wellington Avenue Church, Chicago, 1986

over their faces. They disguised themselves not only to hide from immigration officials, but also because even in Chicago they were in danger of being beaten by local "goons" who punished people who spoke out against the Guatemalan government.

After two years, we were able to bring their children up from Guatemala – a boy and a girl for Ariel and two boys for Maria – and they all moved anonymously into a Northwest Side community in Chicago. Eventually all of the family members became either citizens or legal permanent residents. One of the sons even took medical classes at my university. We took some risks to make it happen, but they took the most risks of all. We broke man's law, but not God's law.

My ministry at Wellington was not only within the walls of the church building. As minister of urban mission, I also headed ecumenical agencies involved in social justice.

When I was appointed executive director of The Institute on the Church in Urban-Industrial Society (ICUIS), it had been dormant for two years, without staff or operations. We quickly grew to a staff of seven, sponsored by national Protestant denominations including

Presbyterians, Methodists, Episcopalians, and my own UCC. We soon added the North American Contact Group of the World Council of Churches, the American Baptist Church, and the Unitarian Universalists as supporting denominations.

Our mission statement declared that we were "an ecumenical agency for strengthening the church in urban-industrial society." We monitored and promoted grassroots urban strategies for economic justice and fostered what were variously called urban ministries, public ministries, and justice ministries. Documenting and preserving history, especially the struggle for social justice, has always been important to me. So my staff and I set about reorganizing the ICUIS files and microfilming its extensive archives on urban ministry efforts in the last half of the 20th century.

In 1985 we published *Justice Ministries: Fighting the War Against Hunger, Homelessness, Joblessness,* to assist churches in creating programs like food pantries and homeless shelters to overcome domestic crises; and *Justice Ministries: The Struggle for Peace, Justice, Sanctuary,* to help churches develop programs like Nuclear Weapon Free Zones and sanctuaries for refugees fleeing the wars in Central America. We provided technical assistance to religious groups in the Playskool lawsuit[1] to alleviate the problems of unemployment from plant closings, in an affirmative action lawsuit for more minority employment in local government, and in the successful campaign to pass the Chicago Nuclear Weapon Free Zone Ordinance. We also developed courses on public ministry and religious leadership training programs.

As ICUIS became successful in promoting social justice, we also became quite controversial. So controversial, in fact, that the board of

---

1   In 1980, the Playskool company received a $1 million industrial revenue bond from the City of Chicago to keep its 700 jobs in Chicago. But in 1984, the plant closed. Supported by religious groups and labor unions, the company was sued by the City of Chicago and forced to provide severance and support of the workers who lost their jobs. Dick Simpson and Clinton Stockwell, eds., *Justice Ministries* (Chicago: ICUIS, 1985), 155-157.

directors – with representatives from the national Protestant denominations – would not allow ICUIS to be directly involved in future social justice projects. When this was mandated, I resigned as executive director, the staff was cut to three, and the organization dissolved a few years later. But even without my role in ICUIS, ecumenical leadership in social justice efforts remained my primary role as an ordained minister. I simply moved on to other agencies and projects.

By the end of the 20th century, those of us at Wellington had in many ways reached the Promised Land. Many of our dreams and visions had been realized. We had taken stands on providing sanctuary to undocumented refugees, and they had now become American citizens. We had supported racial peace in South Africa through economic boycott and protests, and now apartheid had ended. The Cold War with Russia was over; nuclear arsenals were lessening, and the likelihood of worldwide nuclear destruction, while not eliminated, also diminished. The situation in El Salvador and other Central American nations was improving. Reaganomics had ended and a Clinton White House sought to reform welfare, end homelessness, and push for universal health care. It seemed that our vision of peace and justice was beginning to be realized in the world. Because our church came to be viewed as successful, many church leaders envied us, and we were called upon to give advice on social justice actions to others.

But not all was perfect in the Promised Land. Instead of another Harold Washington, another Mayor Daley had come to power in Chicago. Our Chicago schools were a failure, and our shelter in the basement was always filled with homeless men.

Our church eventually became exhausted by our decades-long struggle. We had too few members, too few worshippers, too few leaders. With all that we as a congregation had achieved, we had lost faith in our ability to make our world the way we wanted it to be. Some members had gone from victories to defeat and despair. Some became "burned out" and left the congregation. Unlike King David in the Bible, we had not learned that God is our rock and deliverer.

At Wellington, I preached twice, in different years, on a passage from the Old Testament book of Second Samuel. Around 1000 B.C.E., King David won a number of wars and founded the kingdom of Israel, placing its capital in Jerusalem.

But one of David's sons raped his sister, only to be slain by another son, Absalom. David pardoned Absalom for this deed, but banished him from his presence. In response, Absalom raised a revolt against David, forcing David and his supporters to flee Jerusalem. Family tragedy led to schism and civil war.

While planning their military offensive, David had given explicit orders to his commanders to spare his son Absalom's life. But in the thick of battle, David's commander, Joab, disobeyed orders and killed Absalom. Messengers brought King David the news piecemeal.

The first messenger brought the good news that David's army had won the battle; the revolt had been put down. The second messenger followed with word of Absalom's death. When he heard it, David wept, crying "O my son Absalom, my son, my son Absalom! Would I had died instead of you, O Absalom, my son, my son!"

The Greek story of Agamemnon, who won the great battle of Troy at the cost of sacrificing his daughter to the gods to insure safe passage, is a similar tale. Moreover, he was gone to war for so long that, when he finally returned, his angry wife killed him. Like David, Agamemnon enjoyed great success, but at a very great cost. In this story, Aeschylus teaches the Greek wisdom: Count no man lucky until his life is over and you see the whole of his success and failure, joy and grief.

In my sermons, I encouraged the congregation that there is often loss within success, that deliverance does not erase defeat. Instead, deliverance lifts us to a new height from which we are no longer stuck in old battles. At Wellington, we were still God's people, and we had a role in the world. Our individual challenge was to cooperate with the unique life that was unfolding for each of us, to make a creative contribution, and in so doing, achieve peace with ourselves and satisfaction in our own life.

In 1916, John Dewey wrote: "Democracy needs to be born anew every generation, and education is the midwife."

Across the country, there is a crisis of youth disengagement from politics. This disinterest may stem from the reluctance of teachers to teach "real politics" rather than the dry study of government structures or statistics of behavioralism. When civics is poorly taught, if it is taught at all, the aim is merely for students to be educated enough to vote out of a sense of civic duty. Instead, we need to raise up political leaders who can serve on school boards, organize block clubs, advocate policy changes, or run for public office.

We live in a crucible moment – a time of crisis and change. We need citizen leaders and political engagement to increase democracy and create a more just and perfect union. Among adults, only about 50 to 55 percent of citizens vote. In 2012, only 41 percent of youth voted, although in 2016 the number moved closer to the adult average. For voter participation to change, it must start with our youth.

Studies show that if young people learn to vote, they become lifelong voters. If they learn early to become active in community organizing, they participate for the rest of their lives. But if they don't get involved when they're young, it is much harder to get them to engage later at any level of politics.

This challenge to American democracy and justice will outlast any administration.

Photo: Scott Braam

Encouraging political engagement inside and outside the classroom

16

TEACHING POLITICAL ENGAGEMENT

Students remember little of what they read, hear, or see,
but most of what they experience.

TEACHING POLITICS IS never dull. Particularly not in Chicago, that most political of cities, where there is an endless supply of new political conflicts and revelations. For fifty years, I have brought the struggles of the political world into the classroom and encouraged my students to enter the political arena.

Educating for democracy can be surprisingly controversial. Like my writing, my teaching is not value-free. As a professor, I profess. I seek to educate – to train others to find their own values and to act politically to create greater democracy. That is why I require students to read *The Port Huron Statement* right alongside the *Federalist Papers* and the writings of Edmund Burke, the founder of conservatism.

Teaching politics is controversial because politics, by its nature, involves conflict between political parties, candidates, and groups. The best way to get students to learn is to put the controversy before them and let them choose for themselves. That is also the essence of democracy – a faith that debate and deliberation will lead to better government and better policies than rule by a dictator, no matter how benign.

I wish my approach to teaching political science was the norm. But, oddly, it is not. Political science professors enter the discipline because they are intrigued by politics. But in graduate school, we get trained to be "objective" political *scientists*, like physicists or biologists. We are taught behavioral political science – to be outside observers, not participants.

By contrast, during the late 1960s and 1970s, I was learning politics from the inside – by doing, not just observing from the sidelines. I was an activist, not just a scholar. I practiced real politics, and that is what I helped my students to do.

When I first started teaching at the University of Illinois at Chicago, I was handed a standard textbook and asked to teach introductory American government. Since I never wanted to be a classroom lecturer, I threw out the textbook and wrote *Who Rules?*, a workbook in which students wrote answers to questions about films, lectures, and readings. With my questions as guides, they created their own textbooks and lessons about American politics. As they saw documentary films, met speakers with different points of view, and wrestled with real manifestos and books, they learned much more.

As I injected my practical experiences and insights, my courses became more popular. Instead of lectures and textbooks, I set up direct experiences for students. My courses included films, some of which I made myself; controversial speakers; deliberation in forums like the National Student Issues Convention; simulations; exercises like making an analysis of local government agencies as if students were on a mayor's transition team; and internships with campaigns, government officials, community organizations, or law offices. These teaching methods go by different names such as experiential learning, service learning, civic engagement, and political engagement. But the fundamental goal for me has always been for students to take action, then reflect upon what they did or witnessed firsthand.

There are career downsides to teaching politics rather than duller, less-engaging political science. It is more difficult to achieve promotion and professional recognition. The "publish or perish" mentality in academia is well known. Unfortunately, publishing usually refers solely to peer-reviewed professional journals, instead of books and popular media like newspaper op-eds and articles that can be read by students *and* the general public. Publishing in journals and being politically non-controversial is the direct road to approval and promotion. Picking a purely academic fight within the professional discipline itself by proposing different theories and criticizing existing ones is respected; engaging in public debates is not seen as serious social science.

Some professors are held back from teaching civic engagement by a fear that they might be guilty of indoctrinating their students, just as Mayor Richard J. Daley charged me with "polluting the minds of the young people" back in 1971. But this has been found not to be true. Some years ago, the Carnegie Foundation did a study[1] of 21 political science courses, including my own "Chicago's Future" course. Their rigorous research found that no change in party identity and ideology was produced among the thousands of students taking these courses. They truly were courses of political engagement, not political indoctrination.

In addition to teaching stand-alone courses, I encourage civic engagement to be taught across the disciplines. The goal is to get biology courses to look at policies affecting climate change and English courses to provide tutors in the public schools whose students are faced with broken families, poverty, and challenges of the inner city. I applaud the American Political Science Association for offering their latest book, *Teaching Civic Engagement Across the Disciplines,*[2] free of charge online so that all schools and colleges can better promote civic engagement among all of their students. After all, these students are

---

1   Anne Colby, et. al., *Educating for Democracy: Preparing Undergraduates for Responsible Political Engagement* (Hoboken, NJ: Jossey-Bass, 2007).

2   Elizabeth C. Matto, Alison Rios Millett McCartney, Elizabeth A. Bennion, and Dick Simpson, eds., *Teaching Civic Engagement Across the Disciplines* (Washington, DC: American Political Science Association, 2017).

the current and future citizens who will need to preserve and enhance our democracy.

Practicing what I preach, at UIC I work to coordinate the efforts of the many student groups, faculty, administrators, and institutes who do individual civic engagement projects. We now have a year-round calendar of civic efforts, beginning with the federally-mandated Constitution Day on September 17th each year. One of the most interesting civic efforts of my 50 years at UIC was our attempt to be the site of the Obama Presidential Library, for which we were one of the four finalists. I have invited major legal scholars like George Anastaplo, Cherif Bassiouni, Matthew Lippman, Flint Taylor, Evan McKenzie, and Craig Mousin to speak to us about First Amendment rights, terrorism, government surveillance, abuse by police, constitutional limits on the president, and immigration – real challenges of a living Constitution in our time.

Over the years, I have taught 30,000 students, from freshmen to graduate students. They have been Democrats and Republicans, liberals and conservatives. Some of them have held public office, like Carol Moseley Braun who became a U.S. Senator, an ambassador, and later a candidate for president of the United States. Former students have coauthored books and reports with me; many have served on school boards or become community leaders. They have taught me as much as I have taught them, and I thank and congratulate them all. Hopefully, they will continue to spread the message that we need more democracy and justice than we have yet achieved. And if we are to get it, they will have to lead the fight.

When Harold Washington was elected the first black mayor of Chicago in 1983, many white people feared that the city would fall into Lake Michigan. But in a city with a segregated and racist past, he proved that minorities could run the city at least as well as whites.

Harold Washington's campaign for mayor was highly charged, both politically and racially. Politically, his attempts to reform the patronage system and create non-patronage jobs in city government were a direct attack on the Chicago machine.

Racially, a sense of the emotions involved can be heard in the plea that Democratic Party chairman Ed Vrdolyak made to white precinct workers on the Northwest Side of Chicago, on the Saturday before the primary election: "It would be the worst day in the history of Chicago if your [white] candidate . . . was not elected. It's a racial thing. Don't kid yourself. I'm calling on you to save your city, to save your precinct. We're fighting to keep the city the way it is."[1]

In the general election, after Jane Byrne and Richard M. Daley were defeated in the Democratic Party primary, people for the white Republican candidate chanted *"Epton! Epton! He's our man. We don't want no A-fri-can!"* Race remained central in this election.

Harold Washington prevailed and was Chicago's 41st mayor from April 29, 1983 until his sudden death on November 25, 1987, less than one year into his second term.

---

1   Paul Kleppner, *Chicago Divided: The Making of a Black Mayor* (DeKalb: Northern University Press, 1985), 177.

© Marc PoKempner

Mayor Harold Washington on the campaign trail on Chicago's Northwest Side,
converting whites to become supporters

17

THE HAROLD WASHINGTON YEARS

Even in the middle of conflict, there is a way forward.

HAROLD WASHINGTON WAS a shrewd man with steely idealism that enabled him to enact the many reforms that became his legacy.

My admiration for Harold dates back to his years as a congressman, before he ran for mayor. Twice I invited him to speak to my UIC classes on African-American politics and empowerment in Chicago; the students loved listening to him.

In 1982, when Harold first let it be known that he would run for mayor, I was busy teaching at UIC and attending McCormick Theological Seminary, training to become a minister. Although I had already retired as alderman and was mostly out of politics, I could not pass up the opportunity to be a part of his fledgling campaign. I met with him at his congressional office on the South Side and signed on as a supporter.

Like most political observers, I didn't think he would win. But I did think that it was a battle worth fighting. Of course, I publicly endorsed Washington for mayor; I was one of only two white elected (or formerly elected) officials to do so in his primary run against Mayor Jane Byrne and State's Attorney Richard M. Daley. I also worked to encourage white campaign workers, Latinos, and IVI-IPO leaders to join his efforts.

My first action was to set up meetings between Harold and Puerto Rican leaders, including Rev. Jorge Morales from Humboldt Park. Back when I was an alderman, Rev. Morales and I had worked together on a lawsuit to force the CTA to employ more Latinos. I knew that it would make a huge difference in this race if Harold could get the support of the Latino community.[1] In helping Harold assemble his public relations team, I convinced him to hire Chris Chandler. Chris worked first on Harold's campaign, then in the press office at City Hall. He worked so closely with Washington that he later wrote the book *The Legacy of Harold Washington and the Civil Rights Movement*, for which I wrote the foreword.

Next, I drafted Harold's first two campaign speeches: the announcement of his candidacy at a big rally at a hotel ballroom on 50th Street on the South Side, and his early speech attacking Mayor Jane Byrne's city budget. Harold enjoyed politics and campaigning and was easy to write for. A master wordsmith, he was one of the few charismatic orators who could rival Dr. Martin Luther King, Jr.

While I didn't coordinate the actual precinct work in the campaign, I helped set up the coalitions and press office that helped him win. The campaign became more of a movement than a normal election campaign; thousands of volunteers flooded in, covering the town with "Harold Washington for Mayor" buttons and campaign posters. They registered an extra 100,000 people and got most of them to vote for Harold.

On primary election night, February 22, 1983, hundreds of us packed together in excitement at the McCormick Place Hotel across from the convention center. Rev. Jesse Jackson, Sr. came out early and

---

1   In the primary, Washington ended up receiving only 16 percent of the Latino vote; the remaining 84 percent was split between Richard M. Daley and sitting Mayor Jane Byrne. Even so, the Latino vote provided the mayor's slim margin of victory. In the general election, Washington received over half of the Latino vote. That, along with the support of the black community and progressive whites, was enough to ensure victory.

said, "It's our turn now." That remark would cause problems in the general election, because people interpreted him to mean that blacks would have the only power at City Hall, but it pleased the crowd that night. Harold, himself, came out an hour later, at about 11 pm, to chants of "We want Harold." He let us know that, if we wanted Harold, we had him. And so we did in that primary election – one of the greatest upset victories in the history of Chicago.

Fueled with energy from the primary victory, we went back to campaigning for the general election. On April 12, 1983, Washington defeated his Republican opponent Bernard Epton by the slim margin of 3.7 percent – despite Epton's support from many high-ranking Democrats and their ward organizations. Washington was sworn in at Navy Pier on April 29, 1983. I gave commentary on NBC-TV's live broadcast of that historic event.

Even before his victory, Harold had asked me to co-chair his transition team so we could get his administration off to a strong start. The fact that a blue-ribbon transition team was already in place preparing for a new administration helped demonstrate that he was of mayoral caliber and had the support of well-known civic leaders. Civic leaders I recruited, my students, and I worked tirelessly to produce a 400-page transition team report, *Blueprint of Chicago Government.* It analyzed every single city department and agency and made hundreds of reform recommendations. We proposed issuing a Freedom of Information Executive Order to make city documents easily available to the public, signing the Shakman Court Decree outlawing patronage at City Hall, instituting affirmative action in hiring and contracts, ways to gain control of the Chicago City Council, and hundreds of other major and minor changes.

I later learned that Harold carried a checklist of these transition goals on an envelope in his vest pocket so that he could pull it out and scratch items off the list as they were accomplished. Unlike Mayor Byrne's administration, which threw our transition team report in the wastebasket and kept it secret for nearly four years, Mayor Washington published his and released it at a City Hall press conference.

I considered seeking a role in Washington's new administration, but being on a spiritual path at the time, I decided to be supportive from the sidelines by having him as a speaker at UIC and writing a few draft speeches on the future of Chicago, which he delivered. I met with his department heads now and then to provide specific advice, but mostly I was now a private citizen.

The Harold Washington era was a tumultuous and controversial time, marked by a City Council stalemate which the press dubbed the "Council Wars." But Mayor Washington always found a way of keeping legislation moving. The Council was split 29-21, with the opposition controlling the 29 votes. That meant that the mayor's proposals would usually be blocked. Then opponents would pass a counter-measure, which he would veto, and they had too few votes to override. But finally, a compromise would be reached, and the city would move forward.

The "Council Wars" were not just political; there was also a racial dimension. Washington's opponents were whites, and his allies were blacks, Latinos, and progressive whites. Breaking along mostly racial lines, the battles got very ugly at times. But in the end, many of the changes which we reformers had been proposing for decades were finally enacted.

Among the many achievements of Harold and his administration: he instituted affirmative action in city hiring and contracts, allowed city employees to unionize, and adopted the largest government infrastructure program to benefit neighborhoods in the history of Chicago. While Harold didn't create neighborhood government as I advocated, he definitely created neighborhood empowerment. He transferred hundreds of millions of dollars from patronage workers to community organizations to carry out city services and provide social services. In turn, neighborhood organizations backed the mayor in the council wars battles.

Washington provided hope for those who had been shut out of power and created the opportunity for many of his loyalists to hold positions in government to move a progressive agenda forward for years after his death. Former members of his administration claim that the floor was permanently raised for quality and equality in city government.

On November 26, 1987, Harold Washington suffered a fatal heart attack. When he died, the old Chicago machine was not "dead, dead, dead," as he had so colorfully proclaimed. Traditional patronage still survived. But it was, and continues to be, on the wane.

Beyond his specific accomplishments, Mayor Washington has become a legendary figure who symbolizes what Chicago can become. A black man was, in fact, elected mayor, and two decades later a black man would be elected president of the United States. Going forward, Chicago gained minority school superintendents, police chiefs, and affirmative action in municipal jobs and contracts. Neighborhoods would never again be completely powerless. And despite having a black man at the helm, the city didn't fall into Lake Michigan as many whites had foolishly feared. In short, Chicago was permanently changed for the better by Harold Washington.

I am grateful to have watched this political clash from the inside during such a pivotal time in Chicago's history. Harold Washington's mayoralty was part of the continuing battle between reformers vs. the machine, discrimination vs. integration, and citizen empowerment vs. boss control. The struggles for more democracy and justice for all didn't end with his death. His triumph still serves as an inspiration for those fighting future battles.

Part IV

Interior and Exterior Life

Running for political office may be difficult, but being the spouse of a candidate has its own set of challenges.

Spouses who are normally equal marriage partners are suddenly cast in the supporting role of adoring wife or husband. Not unlike the mother of the groom, they are expected to "put up, shut up, and wear beige." The candidate is in the spotlight; the spouse is just scenery.

They can't affect policy, and no one cares about their opinion – except the media, who will make hay with any differences they sniff out between candidate and spouse.

While the husband or wife is out campaigning, the spouse is on their own to deal with the kids, the bills, and the plumbing problems. Each night they will be greeted by a worn-out partner that doesn't want to rehash all the unpleasantness of his or her day on the campaign trail.

Campaigning is a huge stress on marriages. The higher the office, the more there is at stake. That is why it is crucial for both husband and wife to be completely committed to the endeavor, though neither one can fully anticipate what they are about to encounter.

Sarajane Avidon and me at our wedding, March 22, 1987

18

MARRIAGE TO SARAJANE

*Though they be few, there are advantages
to not being a Cubs fan in Chicago.*

THE CUBS WERE playing that late-summer afternoon in 1986, so most of the guests at my former staff member Rick Kohnen's party were clustered around his TV in the living room. Migrating to the kitchen, I found the only other non-sports-enthusiast at the party: Sarajane Avidon.

I'd known Sarajane since 1970, when she performed in a benefit for Bernie Weisberg's campaign for Constitutional Convention delegate. I got to know her better when she was a precinct captain for my aldermanic campaign in 1971 and had helped organize the entertainment at the 44th Ward Fair we held the next year to celebrate the diverse peoples and talent of our ward.

A 5' 4" character actress with a love for Shakespeare, Sarajane was larger than life. The single name "Sarajane" suited her, although she added her family name Avidon when necessary to put her at the top of playbills and theater posters.

From our renewed friendship in Rick's kitchen, Sarajane and I embarked on a whirlwind courtship filled with adventures and intense conversation. She provided a certain whimsy and creative view of the world which I lacked, and I came to know and love her children, Kate and August. Together, Sarajane and I were each made more whole.

On March 22, 1987, under a chuppah made from purple cloth I had brought back from India, Sarajane and I were married by Wellington Avenue's Rev. David Cheverie and blessed by Rabbi Robert Marx. Seventy friends and family witnessed the vows we pledged to each other in our home on Lunt Avenue.

"I promise to love you, to make time for you in my life, and to be attentive to you when we are together," I vowed. The words my step-daughter Kate recited from Shakespeare's sonnets would resonate with us over the years:

> *Love alters not with his brief hours and weeks,*
> *But bears it out even to the edge of doom.*

We publicly declared, "I am my beloved's, and my beloved is mine." Now it was up to us to make it so. The next two decades would sorely test our love, but it lasted until death did us part.

A month after Sarajane and I were married, I accepted the position of executive director of Clergy and Laity Concerned (CALC), an ecumenical, interfaith organization born out of the Vietnam-era protests and dedicated to leading struggles for justice and peace. I assumed that the emotional support of my new family would enable me to add this responsibility to my teaching and writing load.

CALC enjoyed successes under my leadership. We extended the Chicago Nuclear Weapon Free Zone to include the unincorporated areas of Cook County and suburban towns, we organized the Soweto Day demonstrations against South African apartheid in Chicago, we successfully boycotted Citibank to force its divestment of South African holdings, we opposed contra aid in El Salvador, and we supported the Nuclear Test Ban legislation in Congress.

Even with these successes, finding the funds to continue CALC's activities was an ongoing struggle. The resources of our supporting churches and synagogues were dwindling, and it often wasn't the first cause of its individual donors. I spent countless hours fundraising – hours which soon began taking their toll. Once again, I found myself struggling to achieve balance between the inner and outer dimensions of my life and marriage.

By late 1987, fears began appearing in my journal:

"I have had the repeated worry of my marriage breaking up. This new family has been together more than a year now, and I fear that families may no longer last more than a few years in the society in which we live."

And a month later:

"Sarajane complains that I am not around enough, and when I am, that I am too preoccupied and tired. She says she doesn't know where she stands with me, but by my actions it would seem that she doesn't stand very high."

Through the lens of my fear, the only solution I could see was to relinquish my role at CALC and return my focus to the university, my writing, and my family. I wanted to stay true to my mantra: *new wife, new family, new job, new life.*

When I shared my plans with Sarajane, she thought I was over-reacting, that the solution was too abrupt. Instead, she suggested a halfway measure. Following her advice, I hired an assistant to help with fundraising and scaled back my hours. In the end, even those changes weren't enough to solve the organization's problems or my work overload. I resigned, and the Chicago chapter of CALC eventually collapsed without sufficient individual and denominational support.

The demise of CALC created some breathing room in our life, but it wasn't long before the demands of our house filled in the gaps.

Billed as "the historic Spanjer mansion" by our realtor, our Rogers Park home had been built in the 1920s by an Olympic boxer, which explained the half-gym on the second floor. For all its charm, the tile roof was more appropriate to Spain or Mexico than Chicago winters. Over time, many of those old tiles cracked, causing water damage that eventually brought plaster ceilings crashing down in several rooms, very nearly on our heads. To repair the massive damage, Sarajane used the insurance money to hire crews of actors and set designers, giving them their orders: "Just make sure that it looks good from the third row."

Our Lunt Street home in West Rogers Park

Once the house was restored, we enjoyed several peaceful years in which I taught at UIC, wrote, and became the founding board president of Chicago Shakespeare Theater. Sarajane appeared in a number of plays, including '*Night Mother, Music from a Locked Room, Henry V,* and *Twelfth Night.* But her acting career eventually stalled, and I began to feel the old tug of politics. Which is why, in the otherwise uneventful summer of 1990, we were sitting ducks when my friend Tom Gradel suggested I make a run for Congress.

TOM AND I had known each other since he served as the public relations staff for me and the other reform aldermen in the City Council when I was leader of the opposition bloc. We became friends and allies over the years, as he worked for a variety of political campaigns, labor unions, and community groups. He is a political strategist with unerring political instincts, and I have learned over the years to listen when he speaks. In this case, he had observed a political opportunity which he thought I may have missed, although we had both been mulling over my run for higher office for some time.

When I retired from being an alderman, I hadn't planned to run for Congress, although the possibility lingered in the back of my mind. But I lived in the 9th Congressional District, which belonged to liberal Democrat Congressman Sid Yates. Yates had been in Congress since 1949, and except for a short break in the '60s when he ran (and lost) for U.S. Senate against Senate Minority Leader Everett Dirksen, it looked like his congressional seat was never going to open.

Then came the 1990 redistricting, which merged part of Democratic Congressman Dan Rostenkowski district with Congressman Frank Annunzio's. This put me geographically close enough to the new 5th Congressional District to run in it.

But there was a problem. Although time to file petitions was running out, we still didn't know exactly what the new district boundaries were going to be. If I were to run, would it be against Annunzio or Rostenkowski? But as Tom pointed out, Annunzio had been business partners with political figures who were connected to the mob and had taken political contributions which were clear conflicts of interest.[1] Rostenkowski was a crook, albeit a powerful one (who wouldn't be convicted of corruption until three years later).[2] So we wouldn't really have to know which one I was running against to mount a legitimate campaign. I could comfortably run against either, or best of all, both.

---

1   Details of Congressman Annunzio's crime connections and conflicts of interest are in Thomas J. Gradel and Dick Simpson, *Corrupt Illinois* (Urbana: University of Illinois Press, 2015), 179-181.

2   Ibid., 166-200.

When Tom and I put together a citizens committee to see how much support and funding I would have as a candidate, the results were overwhelmingly positive. If I could assemble a staff adequate to run, he would be my first campaign manager, then transition to public relations and media coordinator. So I faced the question: under these conditions, was I willing to run for Congressman in the soon-to-be redistricted 5th Congressional District?

Sarajane was all for the idea. She strongly encouraged me to accept Tom's suggestion. And why not? The idea of being a congressman, and by extension a congressman's wife, seems wonderful in the abstract. She could just imagine us traveling back and forth to Washington together. And she thought it would be good for me to do something politically exciting again. My step-children, Kate and August, agreed.

As for myself, I was feeling at loose ends. After the excitement of being an alderman, running organizations, being in the newspapers and on TV, addressing crowds – just being a teacher was pretty mundane. And it seemed like a now-or-never moment. If I ever wanted to run, I couldn't wait until Yates retired; he could go on nearly forever. No, this was the one time I was likely to have an opening, while things were still fluid because of the redistricting.

After several kitchen table sessions, Tom, Sarajane, and I came to an agreement. No matter who my opponent would be, I would run in the 1992 Democratic primary.

Gerrymandering is the practice of manipulating the boundaries of a voting district to give political advantage to a party or demographic. It usually benefits incumbents.

In the 1990 Census, Illinois lost enough residents to lose two congressional seats; the districts had to be redrawn. Chicago's new 5th Congressional District was to be carved out of two existing districts. It would comprise the North and Northwest Sides and nearby suburbs.

For Congressman Dan Rostenkowski, that meant losing roughly half of his original district, which was filled with voters who had sent him to Congress since 1959. But being a powerful incumbent, he had influence over how the new boundaries would be drawn.

Once I announced my candidacy, Rostenkowski knew his opponents would be me and Congressman Frank Annunzio, whose district was being eliminated. So Rosty made sure that the map makers drew the new boundaries such that both Annunzio and I lived a couple of blocks outside the new district.

According to the rules, we could run even if we didn't live within the district – as long as we moved into it if elected. Since I lived within a few blocks of the new boundary, and had represented one of the wards as their alderman, I knew the voters would accept me as a legitimate candidate. But if I didn't want to look like a carpetbagger, I would need to move into the district as soon as the election was over, win or lose.

Simpson for Congress campaign button

19

RUNNING FOR CONGRESS

THE FIRST TIME

You can't win if you don't play – and even then,
you still might lose.

WINNING A DEMOCRATIC primary in Chicagoland is tantamount to winning the congressional election. Any Republican opponent would be easily defeated. So even though we didn't know the boundaries of the district, or who I would be running against, we knew that Dan Rostenkowski was going to be the man behind the curtain, one way or another.

During his 30 years in Washington, "Rosty" had become one of the most powerful congressmen in America. As head of the House Ways and Means Committee, he oversaw the nation's tax policy, social security, unemployment, and many other federal government programs. Many people owed him favors, and no one wanted Dan Rostenkowski as an enemy. In Chicago political parlance, he had a lot of clout.

An incumbent with high name recognition, Rosty had previously represented over half of the people in the newly-drawn 5th District, routinely winning with 70 percent of the vote. He was Polish in a district where that mattered. He had a huge war chest. And he had the endorsement of Chicago's popular mayor, Richard M. Daley.

But Rostenkowski had an Achilles' heel: he was corrupt. To win this uphill battle, I would first have to discredit him with the voters.

Once we put our campaign staff together, we began tracking more than a dozen major scandals that Rostenkowski was involved in. Most of them had been covered piecemeal in the media over the last several years. But taken together, they drew a clear picture of a corrupt politician. We compiled all the evidence of corruption we could dig up.

To get media coverage, we knew we had to act, not just speak. So, on November 12, 1991, I staged a press conference to announce my candidacy in front of the Kluczynski Federal Building, then went directly to the FBI to turn over our files on Rosty. It got a lot of media coverage, and my campaign was officially launched.

I had started campaigning early the previous summer with a referendum petition drive to reform Congress, including limiting congressional terms to 12 years. That gave me the opportunity to meet people, get them familiar with my face, and recruit volunteers. We also compiled a mailing list of everyone who signed the petition so we could go back to them in September to sign the formal petition to get me on the ballot.

By late summer of 1991, we finally knew the boundaries of the new district so we could print the nominating petitions to get me on the ballot. I walked door-to-door, street-to-street, and stood at super-markets, bus stops, anywhere I could find people who were voters and residents of the new district. By late November, with more than twice the number of signatures required, I officially filed my petitions with the Board of Election Commission and was put on the ballot without challenge.

In parallel with my negative campaign against Rostenkowski, I advanced a positive progressive agenda. I spoke out on the issues that mattered to voters: women's rights, senior benefits, low-income tax credits, defense over-spending, increasing social services, promoting the arts, and instituting more humane immigration policies. For the most part, my policy stands represented the needs and views of the voters better than Rostenkowski's previous voting record.

The new 5th District was economically conservative, however, with constituents ranging from wealthy to working class. It included many Polish immigrants, some Latinos and Koreans, but few blacks. I spoke to all groups on an equal basis, without falsely appealing to subgroups. I also supported some of the conservative agenda, such as term limits.

For his part, Rostenkowski got busy increasing the amount of constituent services he offered. He opened social security offices and senior centers, continuing to prove that he could bring the pork back to the district.

Over that fall and winter, my life was once again filled with freezing early mornings at 'L' stops and greeting frustrated voters who thought all politicians, including me, were crooks. I faced negative ads filled with outright lies, squabbling campaign staff, volunteers whose arguments I had to settle and whose hurt feelings I had to assuage, and the ever-present demands of fundraising.

Sarajane helped out by appearing with me at all major campaign fundraising events. But mostly she was forced to play second fiddle while I was in the spotlight. Even the staff members weren't much interested in her suggestions or advice. My stepchildren, Kate and August, appeared with me at some press conferences, sat for an oblig-atory-but-fun official family campaign photo taken by a cousin, and, along with my future son-in-law, Jeff Olson, helped distribute campaign posters and open the campaign headquarters.

By late February, I began to see the handwriting on the wall. We had decided early on not to accept any political action committee (PAC) money, and now that decision was really coming home to roost. We had enough money for only one early poll, which showed Rosty in the lead. Naturally, the press accepted that one and their own early polls as definitive. I watched newspaper endorsements to my opponent increase while our bank account dwindled. I knew we hadn't been able

© Susan Reich

Our official campaign photo

to send enough direct mail or buy enough television ads. Most telling of all were the discouraging reports from our precinct volunteers. Our resources were stretched too thin to make a last-minute push. Our only hope was that the voters would elect me on their own.

Election Day began as usual with trips to 'L' and bus stops to greet commuters and urge them to vote for me. Then I began to visit polling places to encourage my workers, although I couldn't make all 500 precincts in a day. I did media interviews when TV or radio stations called. But despite all the months of campaigning and strenuous efforts, Rostenkowski won the primary with 56,059 votes, or 57 percent, to my 41,956 votes. If I had gotten only 14,000 more votes, I would have defeated him in a district of 570,000 people.

ON ELECTION NIGHT, March 17, 1992, I stood onstage at LaVilla Restaurant before several hundred of my campaign workers. In the audience were my family, Sarajane, Kate, and August; close friends; staff members; and people who had supported me since my aldermanic campaign two decades earlier.

I told the crowd that I had called Congressman Rostenkowski

to congratulate him on his victory, but he wouldn't accept my call. I didn't say it, but I assumed that he hated me so much by this stage of our hard-fought campaign that he wouldn't even follow this basic election courtesy and tradition.

I gave a heartfelt thank you to everyone who had sacrificed their time and money for my campaign. I reminded them what our message had been: "Congress should heed the cries of the unemployed and underemployed and those frightened for their future." Even in defeat, I called on Congress to "act now to end the recession – cut the defense budget and reinvest in America…. Heed the cries of the seniors…. Provide justice to victims cheated out of Social Security payments. And act now to provide universal health care." I could make the same speech today and it would still be relevant.

After listing several other injustices, I concluded: "Our people are looking for leaders with compassion and vision to lead them through the current crises. We don't want backroom deals, but a rebirth of freedom, a renewed economy, and a better society for us and our children."

My concession wasn't contrite; it was a call for hope and action. But it didn't change the fact that we had lost.

It was particularly galling to me that I lost to a corrupt opponent. But in the end, the majority of the voters in the 5th District didn't care. They decided to reelect Rosty, knowing full well that he was an "old-style" machine politician. They decided that while he may have been a crook, he was "our crook," who brought back the bacon to our district and our city. His clout was worth more to them than honest and more progressive representation.

When we ran the post-mortem, it struck me that if I could have switched just 7,000 votes, or gotten just 14,000 more of my voters to the polls, I could have won. Or if I had had 100 more volunteer campaign workers to take the campaign message to the voters who didn't show up at the polls. Or if I had accepted PAC money and raised $100,000 more. But I couldn't build a life based on "if only." It was time to fold our tent and get back to normal life. Or so I thought.

In a highly-contested political campaign, it is inevitable that at least one side will use attack ads. Although this has been done since the founding of the republic, it remains a two-edged sword.

On the plus side, negative ads reduce the vote for an opponent. On the minus side, they tend to convince voters that all politicians are crooks. This causes fewer people to vote and reduces citizen participation in elections.

False statements, lies, and innuendos are almost impossible to answer, especially when they are launched late in a campaign. If a damaging direct mail piece lands in voters' mailboxes the weekend before an election, there is no time to refute the charges, regardless of their veracity. If social media or email nano-targeting messages are sent, opposing campaigns usually can't reach the same recipients. If false charges are made in TV ads which cost hundreds of thousands of dollars and take weeks to make, opponents usually don't have the time or resources to respond. This is why successful campaigns have a "war room" to answer attacks before stories can snowball and doom a candidate.

A better approach is to run comparative ads or media statements highlighting different stands or characteristics of each candidate. Nevertheless, there are times in a campaign where nothing but a negative ad will do, such as when you must discredit a powerful opponent who cannot be beaten any other way.

Supporters of the Simpson for Congress campaign

20

RUNNING FOR CONGRESS

THE SECOND TIME

Keep your head in the heat of battle or a split-second misstep can haunt you for a lifetime.

MY FAILED CONGRESSIONAL campaign had stressed us and our marriage in every way: physically, emotionally, and financially. But as unbelievable as it seems in retrospect, within a week I was mulling over whether to run again. I sat down with pen and paper and made a list of my priorities. Only once these were satisfied could I entertain a second run.

At the top of my list was restoring and strengthening my marriage and my role as stepfather to Kate and August. If I couldn't do that, I wouldn't risk another campaign. I didn't want another divorce; twice was bad enough.

Second on the list was selling our home and moving into the 5th Congressional District proper. And with Kate heading off to college soon, it made sense to downsize.

My third priority was to pay off the campaign debt. I dreaded the after-the-fact phone calls ahead of me, begging supporters and donors for more money. But the calls had to be made.

Fourth on my list, I had some damage control to do. My friendship with Tom Gradel had been strained by the rigors of the campaign. We each suffered the natural tendency to blame the other for the loss, rather than feeling gratitude for how close we had nearly come to success. Shortly after the election, Sarajane and I made a point of spending time with Tom and his wife, Corinne, to heal that rift before it could widen. Our friendship continued not only through the next campaign, but for decades to come.

I HAD PROMISED to take Sarajane to Italy no matter how the election turned out. So in May we took off for a thirteen-day trip to Milan, Venice, Florence, and Rome. The night before we were to leave Venice for Florence, a sharp pain in her shoulder kept Sarajane awake all night. We took a water taxi to the Venice Hospital, where she received an X-ray and treatment for an inflamed shoulder. The cortisone shot and a sling alleviated her pain, and we thought the problem was solved. Although we didn't know it at the time, it was an early warning of trouble to come.

When we returned from Italy, we didn't separate as Scott and I had done years earlier, but tension between us remained. It felt like we were mired in quicksand. I hoped a new home would give us a fresh start; at least we were unified in wanting to find a new place to live.

Selling the "Spanjer Mansion" was a challenge, especially since Sarajane was determined to sell for the highest price for which any single-family home in the neighborhood had sold up to then – and boost the property values of our neighbors thereby. With her usual determination, we succeeded. Within several months, we were installed in a classic two-flat home in the Lincoln Square neighborhood.

Although I had lost the primary, I hadn't lost my taste for political work. And the woman who was running for U.S. Senate was a friend. Carol Moseley Braun had been one of my students back in the 1960s, and I had followed her career as a lawyer and elected public official. We had crossed paths often on the campaign trail during the primary election, showing up for some of the same interviews, being endorsed by some of the same organizations. I volunteered to coordinate her campaign on the Northwest Side where I had just run so strongly. At the practical level, it would let me recruit some of her supporters if I decided to run for Congress again.

In an odd twist of politics, because Mayor Richard M. Daley and I both endorsed Carol, I found myself collaborating with the "Daley volunteers," as his patronage worker army called themselves. I found them to be a disciplined group, and there is no doubt that they reached voters that neither Carol's volunteers nor mine could have reached.[1]

© Roberta Dupuis-Devlin, UIC

With Carol Moseley Braun when she announced her campaign
for president at UIC, 2004

---

1   To my great delight, Carol won her Senate race that November to become the first black female senator elected in Illinois. During her term in the Senate, she got entangled in a series of conflict of interest and political missteps which cost her the seat six years later. But she went on to serve with distinction as the United States Ambassador to New Zealand.

I supported Carol's 2004 run for president of the United States by coordinating her issues campaign. I had a smaller role in her 2011 run for mayor, in which she was defeated by Rahm Emanuel.

All through the summer and into the fall, I campaigned for Carol while also working to reduce my own campaign debt. Most of my creditors were patient, giving me some breathing room. Night after night I made phone calls soliciting donations, trying not to get aggravated with people who told me how great I had done in the election but who offered no financial help. We held dinner parties, even a huge garage sale of items from our household and those donated by campaign volunteers, and eventually retired every cent of the debt.

BY LATE 1992, my life had settled down enough for Tom Gradel and me to take stock again. There were plenty of good reasons to make another run at Congress. Personally, I had reached a plateau in my job at the university and had the time and energy to campaign again. Publicly, I was motivated by social causes and the fact that our country had not adopted an urban agenda since Jimmy Carter.

The biggest reason to run was that we had demonstrated that Rostenkowski could be defeated. Before the last primary, he had been winning with 70 percent of the vote. I had reduced that to 57 percent. I knew that, statistically, once I had gotten past 40 percent, all I needed to do was switch 5 percent of the voters to win. In my case, building on my base, it seemed well within reach to pick up another 7,000 switched votes, or get to the polls the thousands who hadn't voted last time but would now that it was obvious that Rosty could be defeated.

So it seemed that there was once again an opportunity to be seized. Tom and I decided that we would gear up now for the March 1994 primary.

When I formally announced my campaign on September 14, 1993, I said, "The purpose of my campaign is not just to weed out one corrupt congressman. It is a campaign to change Congress."

Among the issue positions I announced this time was cutting the defense budget by 10 percent a year for the next five years. I advocated using one half of the $131 billion in savings to improve the economy and create jobs, and the other half to cut the budget deficit and national

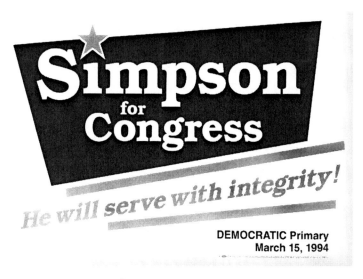

Simpson for Congress campaign poster, 1994

debt. I supported the Equal Rights Amendment, a woman's right to choose an abortion, term limits for congressmen, fairness for seniors whose social security benefits were shortchanged, and more funding for community team policing and public schools.

In my first run for Congress, I did not accept PAC money because I thought being beholden to special interests might limit my ability to represent my district and fight for reforms. Since campaign finance reform was one of the issues on which I ran, it was inconsistent with my message. But now I knew from experience that taking PAC money was a matter of practical necessity. It was simply impossible to amass enough individual donations to mount a winning congressional campaign.

On that basis, I decided to accept PAC money this time – but only from "good PACs" like labor unions, women's organizations, and reform groups. I needn't have worried that it would damage my reputation; no one even questioned the change in my position. But deciding to accept PAC money and actually receiving it are two different things. Very little PAC money appeared because I was too controversial, and, as head of the Ways and Means Committee, Rostenkowski was too powerful. Most of the PACs – especially labor unions – wouldn't risk his wrath when they might need his clout to get their legislation passed. Even liberal PACs didn't want Rosty as an enemy. My compromise decision never gained the additional funds that I had hoped.

Besides being low on funds, there was another fly in the ointment. Because my strong showing in the first race demonstrated that Rostenkowski could be defeated, more ambitious politicians now entered the race. The most significant new candidate was Illinois State Senator John Cullerton, who would later become state Senate president. He was a liberal, traditional Democrat. So now the votes would be split three ways. Seeing this, some pressure was put on me to concede to Cullerton, but I refused.

By November, Cullerton played his hand and the campaign really heated up. Rather than challenge Rostenkowski and his record directly, Cullerton led by running direct mail attack ads against me. Using pictures of me in my clerical robes declaring Wellington Avenue Church to be a Nuclear Weapon Free Zone, he portrayed me as holding weird, new age, cultish views that were out of touch with the people of the 5th Congressional District. To give the impression that the district was in a war zone, he sent empty shell casings to every door. Of course Rostenkowski also ran attack ads, leaving me besieged from both sides. Only later in the campaign did Cullerton also begin to hammer Rostenkowski.

In the middle of this campaign drama, much worse news arrived. Following her shoulder problems during our trip to Italy, Sarajane had been experiencing stomach pain that nothing seemed to alleviate. Tests were ordered, and the diagnosis was delivered. She had a large tumor which would have to be removed by stomach resection.

In December, just as the campaign was entering a critical phase, I took Sarajane to the hospital for surgery. Kate and August joined me for the tense hours in the waiting room. Finally, the news came: the operation was a success. Sarajane was resting in recovery and would be moved to her room in an hour or two.

At that point, I made a misstep that I would regret for the rest of my life. I decided to use those two hours to make a quick visit to nearby Evanston to attend the wedding between two important campaign volunteers. It was essentially a campaign stop. I returned to the hospital soon after Sarajane awoke, but she was justifiably angry that I had left her side at all. No amount of apologizing on my part could overcome the sense of betrayal she felt.

Sarajane's recovery from the resection surgery was much more difficult than we had anticipated. Much worse, however, was what the biopsy confirmed: the tumor was cancerous. We had now entered the separate world of cancer. Aggressive treatment for Sarajane's lymphoma couldn't begin for about six months, until after she had recovered from surgery and adjusted to her new stomach. But the dread of it loomed over us like an ever-present cloud.

The rest of 1993 brought the usual eighteen-hour days of campaigning, press conferences, position papers, bus stops, precinct canvassing, and unrelenting fundraising. Other than our gratitude that Sarajane's surgery had gone well and was now behind us, it was not a joyous Christmas.

Fairly early in the new year, I started to recognize the signs that I could lose the election. In light of Sarajane's cancer diagnosis, I considered dropping out of the campaign. But I couldn't imagine that as a possibility. Well into the campaign already, all of us were overtaken by its sense of momentum. With nominating petitions already filed, press conferences constantly being held, and all the sacrifices made by my family and supporters, I decided it was too late to abandon ship; I would continue the fight.

On February 27, 1994, at a cabaret and dinner fundraising event, I made another misstep. When it was time to speak to the crowd of several hundred people, I introduced Sarajane and thanked her for her support. In an impassioned moment, I declared that if she could fight cancer, we could fight and win this campaign. At this point, very few people knew of Sarajane's illness; you could have heard a pin drop in the room. The second I said it, I knew it was a mistake. Being overcome by emotion and genuinely meaning what I had said was no excuse for playing "the cancer card."

All cancer patients and their families know about "the cancer card." It rightly gives them access to special consideration because of natural human sympathy. This is why a cancer patient and her family might go to the head of a line or be given special reservations and wheelchair service at the airport. But that privilege belongs to the cancer patient alone – it is not something the rest of us can hitch onto.

Subconsciously, I must have known that alluding to Sarajane's cancer would gain more contributions from volunteers and donors. But without Sarajane's permission, I had no right to mention it. In the first place, Sarajane hated the analogy of cancer as a fight; she preferred to imagine herself cooperating with the treatments. And it wasn't my news to tell, especially if I was partially motivated by personal ambition. So tension between us mounted even higher.

As the March election approached, I knew intuitively that we were going to lose. And I was correct. When all the votes were counted, Rostenkowski had won the primary, albeit with less than 50 percent of the vote. Cullerton came in second, and I came in third. In a monument to bad timing, Rostenkowski was indicted soon afterwards and defeated in the November general election by Michael Flanagan, a weak Republican candidate. Flanagan, in turn, was defeated by Democrat Rod Blagojevich, who went on to be elected Illinois Governor – and who, like Rostenkowski, would go to prison for political corruption.

This time, my concession speech felt especially bitter. Losing twice against such a corrupt opponent was a kick in the gut. I was a two-time loser, and Sarajane had ended up with cancer. I felt guilty for not giving her the practical and emotional support she needed during her operation and recovery. I was weighed down with an irrational sense that I should have protected her from contracting cancer. And I worried that, with chemotherapy still ahead of us, my failures would stress our marriage to the breaking point. I determined to do better.

There is a rhythm to cancer, a dark, thudding drumbeat that carries patient and caregiver alike to places they do not want to go. Cycles of anger, despair, fear, hope, and then anger once again. Rounds of diagnosis, treatment, remission, relapse. Patterns of swelling, cutting, healing. Spiking crises followed by endless monotony and staring out of the window, waiting.

This silent rhythm is palpable in the countless trips to the emergency room that are every cancer patient's experience. Brought on by various crises – a blood clot, a high fever, a drop in blood pressure – the visits follow a disinfectant-scented routine that becomes maddeningly familiar.

It begins with the caregiver pulling up at the circular drive in front of the ER, parking briefly to fetch a wheelchair, then carefully wheeling the patient inside, entrusting her to the triage system. Outside again to park before trying to find your way back to the patient through a labyrinth of elevators and corridors. By then the magic words "cancer patient" will have moved the patient up in the queue.

An anxious ER wait is accompanied by blaring televisions, clanking vending machines, and relatives consoling moaning patients. Finally, arrival at a curtained-off room for tests and more tests. Eight hours after arrival comes admittance to the hospital to get the symptoms under control, not to cure the cancer. A week later, patient and caregiver return home to await the next medical crisis.

A favorite of Sarajane's Corgi Cards, this is a depiction of my parents' honeymoon
trip to Pike's Peak, July 1937

21

CANCER'S DARK DANCE –

REMEMBERING SARAJANE

Cancer turns a relationship's cracks into canyons.
Only love can hold it together.

SARAJANE AND I began her 13-year cancer battle with naive optimism. On the strength of her surgeon's declaration that the operation was "a success," we entered her recuperation from stomach surgery with high hopes. Ah, but as we later learned, you can't cure blood cancer with surgery.

In February, a month before the primary election and months after her surgery, the cancer ax fell. Tests showed that Sarajane's lymphoma had spread. There would be no escape from chemotherapy, in her case a cocktail of poisons known to the initiated as CHOP.

But there also seemed to be no escape from the congressional campaign. With only a month to go, I was committed to finishing the race because thousands of people had given me their support in money, work, and votes. Reacting to the news of her diagnosis, Sarajane and I both agreed that I should continue the campaign. But for the next thirteen years I would be driven, not only by love, but also by a sense of guilt that I had not done enough in those critical early months of her illness. As the patient, Sarajane had no choice but to endure cancer and its treatment. She deserved my care, love, and support. After the campaign, I would put my career on hold to care for her, support her, and travel this dark journey with her. But my guilt would not be erased.

Soon after her diagnosis, Sarajane was befriended by a woman whose lymphoma was in remission at the time. She and Sarajane bonded as if they had been to war together. Meeting at a local cafe, they would talk for hours, openly sharing fears, doubts, and where to find the best parking spots near the hospital. They remained close friends until her friend's death several years later.

Despite the support she gained from this friendship, the combination of my campaign and Sarajane's need for me to be physically and emotionally present for her was straining our marriage to the breaking point. When our marital arguments became too frequent and painful, we gained some help from couples therapy. We learned that it was inevitable for some of Sarajane's fears, frustration, and anger to be directed at me, since I was the closest and safest target for her surging emotions. But knowing that intellectually wasn't much comfort while it was actually happening to us. Emotionally, we both felt as though we were being punished for something. Arguments became filled with accusations, and our relationship frayed even further. I turned to the melancholy sounds of Bach's Partitas and Beethoven's final quartets for comfort late at night.

Ironically, the same force that drove us apart also kept us together. We had to depend on each other under the pressure of the disease. Sarajane could not battle cancer on her own, without financial or emotional support. And I loved my wife; I wanted her to be well and content. Underneath the terrible pressure was the bedrock of love we had for each other.

By the end of 1994, Sarajane felt strong enough to audition for the "No Talent Show" on WBEZ. She portrayed the Michigan poet Julia Moore, a favorite of Mark Twain's because of how her doggerel poetry unintentionally parodied the art. Long forgotten, Julia Moore was reborn through Sarajane's live portrayal of her on New Year's Day in a broadcast heard by thousands.

I wish my memories of the next few years were happier, but they were filled with rounds of chemotherapy, marital difficulties, and frequent attendance at funerals for members of our cancer support groups. One of the high points was a blessed period of remission in 1996, when Sarajane felt strong enough to audition for Maria in Shakespeare's comedy, *Twelfth Night*. In his book *Twelfth Night: A User's Guide*, English director Michael Pennington recounted casting Sarajane from her videotaped audition:

> *"Suddenly, Sarajane Avidon pops her head round the edge of an empty frame and whispers urgently, 'Michael Pennington! Sure wish you were here!' Mischief, frustration and eagerness all in a phrase, and she hasn't opened the script yet. Ample and fiftyish, Sarajane is...right for Maria..."*[1]

And she was. Sarajane threw every bit of energy she could spare into her part.

While Sarajane was busy rehearsing, I flew to Austin to visit my parents and check on my father in his decline from Alzheimer's disease. I found him to be more dependent on my mother than ever. But although most things confused him, he could still play a mean gin rummy, and we cherished our last games together.

I returned to Chicago in time to watch Sarajane in what theater critics said was the best performance of Maria they had ever witnessed. Three times I sat in the audience, including her final performance on March 3, the highlight and last curtain call of her acting career.

Now it was our daughter Kate's turn to get married to her fiancé, Jeff Olson. As an ordained minister, I performed their wedding and my friend, Rabbi Robert Marx, gave the Jewish blessing. After a reception in our home, they were off to Uzbekistan with the Peace Corps, working

---

1   Michael Pennington, *Twelfth Night: A User's Guide* (London: Nick Hern Books, 2000), 233.

to change the world together.

In late April, I flew once more to Austin; my father was failing fast. Agitated and confused, he had frequent violent delusions that he was still fighting World War II. His mind seemed to drift back to his Army years, a high point in his life. In fact, he had been a true war hero. As the story went, two soldiers had fallen off a collapsing bridge into a raging river. My father rescued them by lassoing them to safety, Texas style. Later he had been decorated with a Silver Star and Purple Heart for leading his infantry division in the Battle of the Bulge. But that was all behind him now. Despite the confusion of his Alzheimer's disease, he simply chose to stop eating. A week later, I flew back for his funeral.

I returned from my father's funeral to the news that Sarajane's lymphoma had returned. Eight months of chemotherapy had bought less than a year of remission. X-rays and CAT scans showed spots on her lung and leg. A surgeon removed the tumor behind her knee, and this time I stayed for the entire procedure and recovery.

Soon it began to dawn on us that our life consisted of suspended action, broken by the high tension and drama of operations or emergency room visits. Big choices that we might have made, such as my running for department head or Sarajane's wish to move from Chicago to someplace warmer, were repeatedly put on hold until we knew the outcome of each new treatment.

When acting became impossible, Sarajane turned to writing. She and her college friend Susan Sussman co-authored several successful murder mysteries and a play. Graphic art became a new interest, and she developed her collages into "Corgi Cards" which won numerous awards. When she was strong enough to travel, Sarajane and I traded cold Chicago winters for the warmth of Florida. But as the years went by, she was more and more hampered by treatments, declining strength, and the ever-present oxygen tanks.

Sarajane hated being told time and again, after harsh treatments which provided only brief remissions, that her cancer had recurred. It was like getting a death sentence over and over. Surgery, chemotherapy, clinical trials, even a stem-cell transplant – each was supposed to bring a cure. She had stopped smoking, learned meditation, found hidden artistic talent, and had barely begun to feel well again when cancer recurred. It all seemed so unfair. Yet each time, she found the strength to move on, not only with harsher treatments, but with her life, despite ever-greater physical restrictions.

Although our difficulties seemed petty by comparison, the significant others in my support group at the Cancer Wellness Center often talked of being "shelved." Our careers, needs, and hopes were set aside because our sick spouses or children required all of our attention. We had to accept that all plans were tentative, subject to cancellation at any time. Although I was promoted to full professor, published several books, and won some awards, much of my life remained on hold during this dark decade.

Our group also talked about acceptance – of cancer, brushes with death, remissions, and the difficulties in our marriages. We felt that we could meet neither our spouse's nor our own expectations. These conversations were needed to bring perspective and understanding in the darkness. Support groups were essential for both Sarajane and me, but they also brought pain and a loss of our new close friends. In my group, half of the spouses had died by now. Sarajane was nearly the last one left of her original group.

Prednisone, with its accompanying sleeplessness and mood swings, became a virtual third person in our marriage. The more Sarajane suffered its outbursts, the more I wanted to pull back, which only made things worse. The more help she needed, the less she could tolerate our relationship revolving primarily around scheduling and arrangements.

At the end of 2002, our marriage nearly ended under the stress of cancer. Even an emergency session with our couples therapist did not resolve an argument which we had begun the night before over how to load the dishwasher. We became so angry with each other that Sarajane ordered me out of the house. But in her anger, she was also frantic with fear because of new swelling in her face. Before I left, I took her to her cancer doctor, then brought her back home before I packed a suitcase and moved to a hotel. I cried when I left our home, thinking I would never live there again, that my marriage to Sarajane was over.

A day later, Sarajane and I met and struck enough of an uneasy peace that I was able to return home. Our reunion was tense, and I had to face up to just how sick she was. It was time to stop taking outside projects and start taking better care of her, doing a better job of handling the chores at home. She had to take first place.

Unfortunately, even with that moment of clarity, our remaining few years together were punctuated by the same sad cycle of arguments and short separations. Our marital fights constantly revolved around the same issues: Sarajane's insistence that I see her as she really was, yet treat her as an equal even as she grew sicker and more dependent. She hated that I often acted more like her nurse than her husband, but she finally came to the bitter realization that she could no longer handle her health care alone. For my part, I did everything I could to avoid emotional turmoil. Our needs and different temperaments made the journey even more difficult.

Sarajane once expressed her discontent in a letter to me, describing her loneliness, sadness, and anger. Reading it, I felt the same emotions: anger that cancer had shortened and limited her life; fear that she would die, and I would lose her; and frustration that this had happened to us, because we had done nothing to deserve it. Above all, I felt deep sadness to see her and our marriage suffer.

In the midst of Sarajane's medical uncertainties, Lilian, our first grandchild, was born prematurely to Kate and Jeff. Despite her small size and precarious beginnings, Lilian soon grew normally, and Sarajane took great delight in her.

In May 2003, Sarajane needed to travel to San Diego for risky, delicate surgery to remove a blood clot lodged in her lungs. A day or two before the surgery, we shared a good dinner at a San Diego restaurant and drove to a nearby beach to watch the sun set over the ocean.

Then we turned the car around to view a full lunar eclipse – a rare and beautiful sight. We were grateful to share this wonderful celestial moment together.

On the morning of her surgery, I reminded Sarajane once more that I loved her, as did her family and a great many other people. Her last words before the sleep of anesthesia were, "It has been grand."

To all of our relief, Sarajane not only survived the surgery, but by July her breathing had improved so much that she was off oxygen altogether. She still faced operations, treatments, and the accompanying depression and anxiety. But we were grateful for the respites when they came.

* * * * *

Courtesy of Chicago Shakespeare Theater

Sarajane Avidon and other cast members of Chicago Shakespeare Theater's inaugural production of Henry V on the roof of the Red Lion Pub in August 1986

Remembering Sarajane

IT TOOK A decade to clear the cobwebs, but I now see my 19 years of marriage to Sarajane in a happier perspective. Her illness and death is still a powerful, searing memory, but it no longer dominates my recollections of her.

Sarajane succumbed to cancer on March 29, 2006, just a few months shy of her 65th birthday. Her memorial service, a last bow, as it were, was attended by more than 200 people at Chicago Shakespeare Theater. A smaller memorial was held in Parkersburg, West Virginia, where most of her ashes were placed in the family grave alongside her parents.

Those final months were difficult for Sarajane, undergoing a lung biopsy, chemotherapy, and finally, hospice care. Her peace was interrupted by many trips to the hospital as we made every effort to stop the lung cancer which had developed. We struggled to accept the truth: after all her bouts with lymphoma, it was the lung cancer that was incurable. She was dying for real this time, with no reprieve.

A morphine drip relieved some of the pain, and a caregiver helped with the nearly round-the-clock care. We weren't yet overwhelmed with sadness because we didn't believe the end would come quickly.

In early March, Margaret England, Jeff's mom and Kate's mother-in-law, who was a hospice nurse, suggested that we begin home hospice care for Sarajane. Once Sarajane's doctors agreed, we made the arrangements.

I recall one evening during that time of waiting that brought an overwhelming mix of experiences and emotions. With both a friend and her hospice caretaker attending to Sarajane, I broke away to make a presentation at Elmhurst College that I had agreed to give months earlier. Incredibly, Wayne Shull, my boyhood best friend from Houston, was in town and attended the dinner and lecture. Afterwards, we spent a quick hour at a nearby coffee shop trying to catch up on 30 years of separation before I rushed back to Sarajane's bedside. It was an evening of highs and lows, triumph, joy, and grief all piled on together. Life was like that in the cancer years.

On March 22nd, Sarajane and I celebrated our 19th wedding anniversary by sharing a flute of Champagne at her bedside. In sickness and health, in sadness and joy, we had lived together until death, in fact, did us part. It was a bittersweet moment in which we said I love you one last time and remembered the goodness of our life together.

During her final days, more than twenty family members and friends came to say their farewells. Our daughter Kate even set up a Google chat group called "IloveSJ" so we could report on her situation and people could send her encouraging messages. Though she was on morphine, Sarajane was able to chat coherently and be lifted by her friends' love and support. She was particularly delighted by the visits with her grandchildren, four-year-old Lilian and baby Paula. She hoped Lilian would remember her; it saddened her to think that little Paula was too young to do so.

Now everything seemed to be happening so quickly. Within weeks, we had gone from Sarajane in the hospital, to home health care, to hospice care, to me making life and death decisions for her. But she was true to her spirit to the end. Even through the illness and drugs, she was effective in communicating her wishes. Sarajane controlled the ending of her own tale.

Four days before her death, Sarajane was still receiving visitors. Margaret came and sat in the bed next to her with baby Paula in her arms. They took turns holding the baby and singing children's songs to her. When Margaret bounced Paula and sang "She wore an itsy, bitsy, teeny, weeny, yellow polka dot bikini," they all got the giggles. That was the last time we heard Sarajane laugh with abandon.

We cried three times together during her last waking days. The first was when I played the tape of a special concert recorded just for her by the Old Town School Women's Chorus. Sarajane was a proud member of the chorus and had loved singing with them. I would weep again when they sang with the angels for Sarajane at her memorial service.

When Sarajane's closest girlhood friend called to say farewell, we cried again.

And when a letter came from old friends on the sad fate of New Orleans after Hurricane Katrina, which somehow paralleled Sarajane's rapid decline, we wept a third time.

On her last lucid night, I read aloud every single email posted by the "IloveSJ" group, including the bad actor jokes and virtual lunches and teas that her friends had described for her. We also read the messages Sarajane had posted. She let me know that the most important message was this: "Sarajane loves Dick, August, and Kate." She didn't want the three of us to ever forget that.

Once she slipped into a coma, music eased her passage. The hospice sent a harpist to play for her, and I often played the songs her chorus at the Old Town School had sung for her. She passed peacefully on March 29, 2006, finally relieved of the terrible pain.

OUR FRIEND JUDY Peres wrote this in Sarajane's Chicago Tribune obituary:

Even on her deathbed, Sarajane appreciated a bad joke. What else would you expect from the irrepressible actress who couldn't eat at an expensive restaurant without hanging a spoon on her nose [which she taught her children and grandchildren to do so the family tradition continues].

Her friends...in her last days...regaled her by sharing inanities on an Internet club called "I love SJ"... How many actors does it take to change a light bulb? Just one: He stands there and the world revolves around him.

Sarajane ended her last letter to us with the following lines:

So Long, It's Been Good to Know Ya.
My mother thanks you,
My father thanks you,
And I thank you.
Hugs and kisses,
Sarajane Avidon

Part V

The New Normal

From 1991-2002, Sierra Leone suffered a long and brutal civil war. It began when the Revolutionary United Front (RUF), with support from Liberian President Charles Taylor's National Patriotic Front, attempted to overthrow Sierra Leone President Joseph Momoh's government.

Early on, the RUF took control of the east and south, which was rich in alluvial diamonds. The government's weak response set up a military coup in April 1992. During the ensuing fighting, other forces became involved until in May 1997, a disgruntled group of officers in the Sierra Leone Army staged another coup. World leaders eventually intervened. With the help of a UN mandate, Guinean air support, and the British, the RUF was finally defeated.

Both rebel forces and government troops committed horrible atrocities against civilians during the war. They were used as child soldiers; human shields; forced into labor; their arms, legs, ears, and lips were cut off; and women were raped.

By the time the conflict officially ended in January 2002, it was estimated that at least 50,000 people had died, hundreds of thousands were affected by the violence, and 2,000,000 were displaced.

May 2002 brought post-war elections. The new administration began the long road back to reconciliation, economic recovery, and reform. A decade later former Liberian rebel and president Charles Taylor was found guilty at The Hague of war crimes and crimes against humanity committed during Sierra Leone's civil war.

The Sierra Leone national amputee soccer team, 2008

22

BACK TO AFRICA

There is great fulfillment in following a road not taken.

BURNED OUT SHELLS of aircraft still sat near the runway of Lungi Airport when I landed in Sierra Leone in 2008. In fact, the plane on which I rode had a number of amputees whose limbs had been hacked off by child soldiers during the war. But the Sierra Leoneans I met throughout my stay were as friendly and welcoming as ever.

After Sarajane died and I was able to travel again, my mind wandered back to Sierra Leone. When Scott and I had visited there in 1966, I thought I had found my life's passion, the path of Africa and African studies. But early in the 1970s, I became enmeshed in American and Chicago politics and stopped publishing, studying, or teaching about Africa.

Over the years, I had mostly lost track of what was happening back in Sierra Leone, other than following reports of the terrible civil war that had begun in 1991.

But now I was bedeviled by questions: how could things have gone so wrong in Sierra Leone, a country that had seemed so primed for economic development and democracy? If I went back to Africa, I thought I could pick up the road not traveled forty years earlier. So, I returned.

As often happens in life, once the decision was made, the necessary stepping stones appeared to make the journey possible. Though I had no remaining contacts in Sierra Leone, I discovered there was a Sierra Leonean history professor, Joseph Bangura, teaching at Kalamazoo College, a mere four-hour drive from Chicago.

Joseph and I began a correspondence which soon became a friendship. He connected me with some of his former Fourah Bay College classmates, now the Dean of Social Science and Law at Fourah Bay College, and another who was an official in the Sierra Leonean Department of Education. One agreed to meet me upon my arrival at Lungi Airport and the other arranged my stay in Freetown.

Freetown, Sierra Leone

I was filled with questions of how Sierra Leone had become a "failed state," the causes of their civil war, and how their once-promising democracy had failed. These questions were partially answered in the half-dozen books I read on the subject and by my interviews with former government officials and scholars in country. But then I was left with a new and more urgent question: Could Sierra Leone now achieve democracy and healthy economic development? I determined to find out.

On Memorial Day, 2008, I left Chicago for my two-month stay in Sierra Leone. In some ways, it was a journey without a map. I didn't know what I would find in Sierra Leone, or what I would discover about myself.

My first discovery occurred on the flight itself. I was privileged to travel with some members of Sierra Leone's national amputee soccer team, who had been playing exhibition matches in Europe. Each of these young men had lost a limb during Sierra Leone's eleven-year civil war when rebel soldiers had cut off one of their arms or legs, then released them, knowing they would be unable to fight. But once their country had survived the war and their wounds had healed, they started training to play the fast and furious game of soccer.

Halfway through my stay in Sierra Leone, I visited their practice field at Lumley Beach to interview and photograph these amazing young men. I would later use that photograph on the cover of my book, *African Democracy and Development,* as a fitting symbol of their country. The striking image of amputees playing professional-level soccer, despite the handicaps created by the brutal civil war, is also a symbol of the resilience of their nation.

Sierra Leone had suffered greatly in the forty years since I had last visited. Under President Siaka Stevens's administration from 1971-1985, a centralized one-party state had formed. He was shrewd enough to rule effectively, but his successor, Joseph Momoh, was indecisive and incompetent. Corruption, greed, flawed decisions, and harmful international economic policies beyond Sierra Leone's control led to economic decline and political oppression. This, in turn, led to civil war when Sierra Leone, already rotted from within, suffered from an external attack by rebels in 1991.

As the world now knows, the drug-influenced rebel soldiers became evil incarnate with killings, rapes, looting, amputations, and the making of child soldiers. They eagerly sought "blood diamonds" for their own greed and to fuel their war. When this evil was loosed, civilization did not hold.

After the war finally ended in 2002, Sierra Leone struggled mightily to rebuild through a Truth and Reconciliation Commission and an International Tribunal (which would eventually convict Charles Taylor and other war criminals). But the country still had to repair its roads, reestablish electrical service, and create better lives and economic opportunities for its citizens.

Despite these challenges, the Sierra Leoneans were remarkably hopeful about their future. Perhaps they thought that they had seen the worst, that things could only improve for their beloved "Salone." Throughout my stay, they declared, "Never will we go back to being a one-party state or to civil war." It is on that basis that they worked to rebuild their lives and country. The 10,000 amputees among them, including those on their national soccer team, visibly remind them every day of the horrors of war, how far they have recovered, and how far they have yet to go. And after my visit, they would face the further challenges of an Ebola epidemic and mudslides in their capital, Freetown.

When I was ready to begin my research, Professor Osman Gbla of Fourah Bay College set me up at his research institution in downtown Freetown. Unlike in 1966, there were now computers, limited Internet access, and ubiquitous cell phones. But electricity was still sporadic and unpredictable. Some of the government-owned generators were installed as long ago as 1948 and copper wire power lines from hydroelectric power plants were often cut down and stolen for scrap by vandals.

Through the kindness of Professor Bangura's connections, I was given access to the highest levels of Sierra Leonean government in Freetown. Every day, as much as I was able, I met with high government officials including the vice president, members of Parliament, and former cabinet ministers. I undertook research at the library and talked to faculty and students at Fourah Bay College. I sat in meetings with civil society leaders at the research institute. I started with my basic questions and filled in the answers as people told me about the past and their hopes for the future. As I talked to people with first-hand knowledge at all levels of society and compared their answers, a consensus history emerged.

Back home, on June 6, the *Chicago Sun-Times* published my op-ed entitled "Obama's Candidacy Brings Hope to Africa." In it I quoted a number of Sierra Leoneans, including a research institute staff member, Alimamy Conteh. Conteh believed it would be joyous if Barack Obama won the presidency because "his heart is with West Africa." He hoped that Obama would bring a change from the policies of the Bush administration and spend less of America's wealth on the war in Iraq, and more on Africa. Sierra Leoneans hoped for an American administration that would join their struggle against disease, war, and poverty – for an American president who cared about them. They believed that Obama would be their president as well as ours.

On July 5, as an international election observer for the Sierra Leonean local government elections, I was allowed to see local

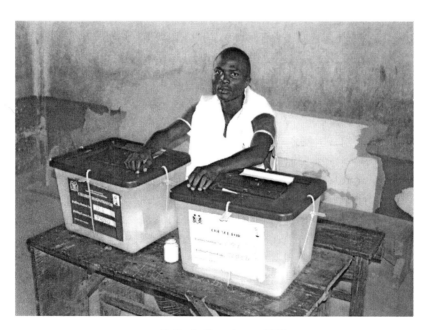

Voting in Sierra Leone, 2008

government in the process of being reestablished after the war. I began the day by observing the election in Freetown, then drove the rough highway to upcountry Kenema. There I discovered that a much smaller cinema, bar, and dance hall had replaced the large movie theater where Scott and I had watched Italian westerns forty years earlier. The same evening, I was able to meet with all the candidates for mayor and understand what was at stake in this first election of local government officials in decades. Democracy at the grassroots was being replanted.

The local government election in Kenema was held mostly in school buildings, and conducted fairly, according to international standards. Despite sometimes having to wait in lines to do so, the Sierra Leoneans voted in greater percentages than we Americans typically do.

In exploring Kenema, I found that there was still only one paved road. The few stores I saw were dealers buying diamonds which had been dug further upcountry. A traditional open-air market still flourished several days a week, but there was no real industry since the furniture maker closed years ago. Side streets were made of washboard dirt, best traveled by jeeps and Land Rovers.

Although I had enjoyed access to the highest levels of Sierra Leonean government and society, I experienced great difficulty arranging a meeting with anyone at my own American embassy. When I finally secured a meeting with the cultural attaché at his office, I agreed to provide him with my full report on the problems of Sierra Leonean local government. I was disappointed to learn that the report I submitted to him upon my return had no more practical effect than most of my transition team reports for Chicago officials. No reforms followed from it. Likewise, the report that I gave the country's vice president, at his request, on modernizing Sierra Leonean local government went unimplemented.

Everything in Sierra Leone moved more slowly than my American expectations. Laundry took an extra day to dry because of rain and humidity. Meetings always started an hour late. Checks on U.S. banks took six weeks to clear. I learned to "make haste slowly," and determined to bring that lesson back to Chicago with me. As I took the long ferry ride and the longer plane ride home to Chicago, I was saddened to leave Salone, with its beautiful beaches and optimistic people, undefeated by war and disease.

I returned home with my initial question unanswered. Perhaps it would be possible for Sierra Leone to achieve a positive democracy and economic development, but the challenges ahead of them were enormous. I looked for ways to help this country that I had come to love. Through my Illinois congressmen, I pushed to send the Peace Corps back to Sierra Leone.[1] I connected with the wonderful organization Books for Africa and became their Sierra Leone coordinator. We have since sent back over 350,000 books to replenish school, university, and public libraries destroyed by the war. During the Ebola crisis, I helped support another charity, Schools for Salone, in its efforts to provide 7500 radios to help get health information and school lessons out to villages. And I began working with Sierra Leonean scholars to publish books on "failed states" so that the civil wars and difficult process of recovery could be better understood.

---

1   Peace Corps volunteers were finally cleared to return to Sierra Leone in 2011, after an absence of 16 years.

Dating over 65, like getting old, is not for sissies.

Whether it be from death or divorce, if we find ourselves alone, even a "successful" life can feel hollow, even pointless. We want someone to share it with.

So how to find someone new at our age? Dating is so different from how it was 50, 30, or even 20 years ago. Instead of blind dates and sock hops, we are offered "gray dating" apps, which many of us refuse to use.

Even the way we relate to one another has changed. Who opens the door? Who pays for dinner – the person who can best afford it? Or do we split the tab? And who makes the first move? At our age, we can't afford to be too shy or wait forever. Add in fear of rejection and the baggage we all carry, and we can become leery of dating at all. And who remembers how to flirt at our age?

But we're just people, all longing for the same thing: real connection with another human being. Caring, kindness, and touching are always in style.

So, we get out there and make the effort. We go to concerts. We volunteer. We join protests. Sometimes, without planning it, we meet someone when we least expect it. We fall in love again. That's worth the risk, at any age.

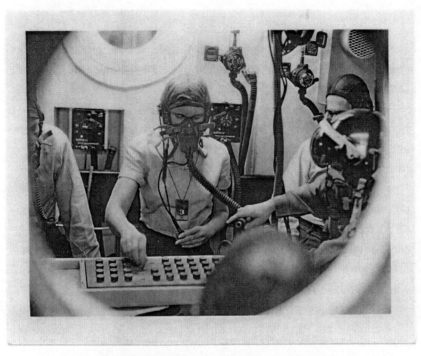

Dorothy Storck in training to be an astronaut, 1985

THE REMARKABLE DOROTHY STORCK

It's tempting to run when romance confronts real life, but love stays put.

THE LAST THING I wanted was to be disloyal to Sarajane's memory. As she was dying, she predicted a long line of women hoping to snare me with casseroles and sympathy. That didn't happen. For my part, I had more or less planned to stay single and alone. But that didn't happen either.

After Sarajane's death, I entered a period of manic energy. I traveled to Africa, organized national and international conferences, published books, and found myself head of the Political Science Department at UIC.

After an IVI-IPO meeting one night, I stopped in at a political dinner party at my friend Don Rose's home. There I became reacquainted with Dorothy Storck, a retired journalist who I recognized from her columnist days in Chicago in the 1970s.

Dorothy and I were soon dating, and much to both of our surprise, our love flourished. For a long time, she hid from me that she was 13 years older – she was 78, and I, 65, when our late-life romance began. But somehow we made it work, even when cancer became an unwanted part of our lives.

Dorothy Storck was a heroine who broke glass ceilings, a Pulitzer Prize-winning columnist who reported from around the world. Stylish and gorgeous even as she grew older, she adorned every outfit with her collection of beautiful Hermès scarves and jewelry from ports of call around the world. Her wit and sometimes-sharp tongue could have earned her a spot at Dorothy Parker's Algonquin group in years gone by.

For readers around the world, Dorothy wrote straight to the heart. She was a walking repository of the most important events and personalities of the late 20th and early 21st centuries, reporting on stories which are now in our history books. She covered the 1968 and 1972 presidential campaigns, the trial of Sirhan Sirhan who assassinated Robert Kennedy, the Detroit riots, Americans in Mexican jails, the space voyages of Apollo 10, 11, and 13, and the anniversary of the Apollo missions 40 years later. She and Walter Cronkite trained with NASA to be the first journalists in space before the 1986 failure of the Challenger Space Shuttle ended their program of sending civilians into space. What a story she would have written had she blasted off into that vast unknown universe.

Dorothy's social life was equally dramatic. She was once engaged to Milton Berle, and for a short while she even dated Richard Cain, the crooked former Chicago cop who was later killed by the mob. She was close friends with Chicagoan Mike Royko, who once told her that she was the only columnist who threatened his preeminent position as the best columnist in Chicago. Their columns and papers are now together at the Newberry Library in Chicago for future generations to enjoy.

Early in her career as an Air Force major, Dorothy's pragmatism got her into hot water. When too many women in her command were becoming pregnant, she provided them with information on birth control, which did not sit well with either the Catholic chaplain or the Air Force. As punishment, she was sent to an air base in Alaska where she became a squadron commander of 400 women.

From Alaska, her job as a public relations officer for the military eventually brought her to Chicago. It was here that she left the armed forces to become a journalist for $95 a week, her way of protesting the military's lies which she helped uncover about the Vietnam War.

Dorothy began her newspaper career writing for the old *Chicago American*. In the '70s she joined *The Philadelphia Inquirer*. By the time she left Philadelphia for London in the '80s, her column was syndicated to 250 newspapers.

Dorothea, her real name which she preferred I call her, returned to Chicago in 1991, because she could afford to live here in style and be near her old newspaper friends. Upon her return, she noticed a change:

> *"The city seemed to have burst out of its old workman's coveralls into some kind of Green Giant garb…. You got the feeling flying in, seeing that soaring rim [of high rises] with the flat bungalow neighborhoods stretching to the west that one day Chicago might just capsize like a ship leaning too far port. Walking up Michigan Avenue now, I feel a sense of lushness and bustle, of wildness… This is a town of low-down blues rising up from cellars and street corners."*

When blogging became popular, Dorothy gave it a try, then abandoned it. She enjoyed stirring up a hornet's nest with controversial topics, but after so many years as a newspaper woman, she could not be convinced that blogging was a legitimate form of publication. You couldn't hold it in your hand like a newspaper, and you didn't run into readers who complimented you.

About four years after Dorothea and I had become a couple, she developed backaches that trips to the chiropractor could not cure. A spinal tap revealed myeloma. I immediately understood what that news meant, maybe better than she did. I also knew that I would travel the cancer road with her just as I had with Sarajane.

For five years Dorothea endured chemotherapy, holding my arm and using her beautiful carved wooden cane to provide balance as we walked down endless hospital corridors together. On days when

Vacation in Spain, 2010

her treatments weren't too difficult, we would dine at a faux British pub which ever-so-faintly reminded Dorothea of better days as a correspondent in London.

Eventually trips to the emergency room and hospital stays increased. Visits to her apartment and the drug store became more frequent; a morphine patch was added when simple pills no longer eased the pain. In August of her 88th year, Dorothea's long and adventuresome life came to a close.

ON A BREEZY September day, Dorothea's ashes and I made it through the TSA security checkpoint at O'Hare. We were free now to take our last journey together, flying above white scattered clouds like angels are said to do. Her sister, brother, nephew, and I buried her with full military honors at West Point, where she rests next to her military father and former actress mother.

The next few years saw a City Council memorial resolution, the creation of the annual Dorothy Storck award by the Chicago Journalist Association, and her columns safely deposited at the Newberry Library.

Sailing is a good metaphor for the years Dorothea was my fiancée. We never married nor lived together in the same home; after my previous marriages, I didn't want to do so. But the ring I gave her was a symbol of the commitment we shared until her death. And although we were from different worlds, we were content to sit together on the tall ship on which we traveled. I still cherish the lines she wrote in a piece entitled "Sail Away":

> *"Let them whinge who will, when those sails billow up in starlit sky, when the wind is in your face and the sea salt is on your tongue . . . As twilight falls on Grace Kelly's palace and the lights flicker on the chateaux in the hills, I am content to sit still on my tall ship. Tomorrow is Cannes and the end of the voyage. It has been a good one."*

Spain, 2010

In academia, there exists a false tension between scholarship, on the one hand, and activism, on the other. But activism is, in fact, a fundamental element of higher education. A professor should, literally, profess the truth as best he or she knows it. And if the surest way to truth – especially about society and politics – is debate between at least two points of view, then activist academics are sorely needed in the public arena.

Activist academics, sometimes called public intellectuals, contribute to public debate about government and societal policies and problems. They do not simply observe from the ivory tower. They do not merely teach about people and politics. Instead, they work to change the world via advocacy, organizing, and action.

These academics live in tension with the broader accepted goals of colleges and universities, which are to follow the holy trinity of research, teaching, and service. They are often at a career disadvantage because institutions tend to fear that their ideology will influence and bias research and teaching – that instruction will become indoctrination. But in fact, these activities enhance professors' ability to convey course content to their students. Seeing political processes from the inside allows teachers and scholars to understand them first, and prove their conclusions later, and thus to help fix what is broken in our politics and communities.

The School of Athens, fresco by Raphael

24

ACTIVIST ACADEMICS: FRED HESS, PIERRE DEVISE, AND WOODY BOWMAN

When joined with activism,
academic studies can transform society.

I HAVE HAD as colleagues and friends a number of academics of my generation who tried actively to shape a better world. A small minority, they were often chided for not being academic or scholarly enough, for letting their passion for the public good affect their research and teaching. But for me they were important friends and allies.

G. Alfred (Fred) Hess was one such person. A tall, fit man who enjoyed tennis and carried himself with a quiet reticence, he combined his early role of preacher with lifetime roles of teacher and civic leader.

Fred and I first became friends because of our shared roots in the Institute of Cultural Affairs in Uptown, an offspring of the Christian Faith and Life Community to which I belonged back in Austin, Texas. We shared many of life's ups and downs, and he often guest-lectured to my "Future of Chicago" class. Students loved him because he was so passionate about creating a better future, fixing Chicago's broken school system, and helping our children.

Fred was a research professor of education and social policy at Northwestern University. In his courses, he used anthropology to study our current society, especially schools and education, just as other anthropologists might study tribal societies.

In the job which launched his civic career, Fred became the head of the Chicago Panel on Public School Finance. In that position, he led and chronicled the Chicago School Reform effort under Mayor Harold Washington, which empowered local school councils to guide their individual schools within Chicago's massive public school system. He wrote later in his book, *School Restructuring, Chicago Style*, that he was "just one of this throng of people involved in creating the reform movement."[1] But, in truth, as the one-man secretariat of the movement, he kept the enduring record of what happened and lived to evaluate its successes and failures a decade later.

Fred's experience began "as fairly traditional, detached research on the problems and difficulties of the school system."[2] It eventually evolved into a passionate effort to help turn around a system that was horrifying in its failure to provide an adequate education to the city's public school students. He, himself, was transformed from an objective social scientist into a passionate advocate.

Fred's solution to school problems were practical: more democratic control through local school councils, better principals with strong leadership skills, more emphasis on order and discipline. He recommended that administrations focus on student attendance, improve student pass rates, use active instructional techniques that emphasize interaction with students, and assure that the school buildings looked cared for. He advocated teacher and staff retraining, more student responsibility for learning, and more parental involvement. The remedies weren't rocket science, but they came from careful study of

---

1   G. Alfred Hess, *School Restructuring, Chicago Style* (Thousand Oaks, CA: Corwin, 1991).

2   Ibid.

dozens of succeeding and failing schools. His solutions were partially implemented in Chicago, Evanston, Philadelphia, and around the world. Unfortunately, they were rarely fully implemented, and our public schools continue to flounder.

Fred was motivated by a fierce spirit of social justice, and his passion moved and inspired others. As a civic leader, he had neither public office, government authority, nor great wealth. But by dint of hard work, reason, and persuasion, he was able to change schooling in Chicago for the better. Fred passed away in 2006, at age 68.

Pierre deVise taught with me at UIC and then later at Roosevelt University. Different in temperament from Fred, he was more outwardly intense and retained a strong accent from his native Belgium, even after decades of living in the States. Pierre was a University of Chicago-trained demographer who, unlike most academics, was very public-relations savvy.

For several decades running, Pierre opened my "Chicago's Future" lecture series each fall with lectures on race and wealth inequality in Chicago. To this day, I begin the public talks with a Pierre deVise Memorial Lecture given by a major social scientist.

Pierre was famous for branding Chicago as the most segregated city in North America, and he had the statistical data from the U.S. Census to back up his claim. His book, *Chicago's Widening Color Gap*, remains influential in its impact.

Pierre did his research the old-fashioned way, before computers made the work of demographers easier. In his famous 1967 study of the Chicago metropolitan region, he copied census data for each of the 250 community areas onto index cards and ordered them by hand from the richest to the poorest, based upon three or four factors. Pierre then plotted the ten richest and poorest communities on a map. The ten poorest communities were essentially the all-black neighborhoods around Chicago Housing Authority projects like the Robert Taylor Homes. The ten richest communities, like Kenilworth, were in all-white suburbs north and west of the city. The colors on his map graphically illustrated that wealth and race were correlated as a result of residential segregation.

Doing this study cost Pierre his job as an urban planner at the Northeast Illinois Planning Commission, but he came to UIC as a faculty member where, as colleagues, we rallied against Chicago's segregation. In the five decades following his ground-breaking study, the segregation index has improved in Chicago, but the wealth inequality – the "color gap" between rich whites and poor blacks in segregated neighborhoods – has only widened.

Pierre was his own one-man public relations firm. He got better media coverage of his studies than almost any other scholar I knew. He would do complicated studies, but then repackage them as press releases with controversial and provocative claims (such as Chicago being the most segregated city in North America). He would personally deliver them, often by bicycle – before the current cycling fad – to the newsrooms of the major newspapers who would then trumpet them the next day with major in-depth and, sometimes, front page stories which the other media would be forced to cover.

Pierre died in 2004 at the age of 79.[3] In his obituary, the Chicago Tribune described him as "the Windy City's Socrates: a free-spirited intellect who chronicled Chicago's ever-changing neighborhoods in a manner guaranteed to provoke outrage from conventional professors and thin-skinned politicians."

Woods (Woody) Bowman was another activist academic I knew well, liked, and admired. In the early 1970s, Woody was an assistant professor in economics at UIC who became an adjunct associate professor while he served seven terms in the state legislature. He later went on to teach at DePaul University for more than two decades.

---

3   Pierre deVise's papers are archived in Special Collections at UIC's Richard J. Daley Library.

Woody was part of the movement of independent politics on Chicago's North Side and the nearby northern suburbs. While representing Evanston and Chicago's Rogers Park neighborhood in the Illinois House, he continually tried to break the control of machine politics. Because of his background in economics, he was appointed to serve on the House Appropriations Committee. Later he was appointed CFO of Cook County and remained an active economic advisor in Cook County politics until his death.

What those of us in reform politics remember most is how Woody remained true to the independent movement throughout his career. Some reformers were co-opted by power or by the powerful, but Woody remained true to his ideals.

When Woody was killed in an automobile accident in the summer of 2015, he had only recently retired. He and his wife, Michele, were to meet me the next week so they could contribute more than 200 books to help replace those lost during Sierra Leone's civil war. Later Michele did donate those books in his memory, and they have now formed the backbone of the library of the Institute of Public Affairs and Management in Freetown, Sierra Leone. Hopefully they will help educate future public servants – future Woody Bowmans – in Sierra Leone.

IN THEIR DIFFERENT ways, Fred, Pierre, and Woody embodied the reform spirit of our 1960s generation. They saw evils in society which they were able to document and prove. They proposed solutions which proved difficult to get adopted. Yet decade after decade, these activist academics remained true to their causes. Without their dedication and advocacy, our society would be the poorer.

Chicagoan Saul Alinsky literally wrote the book on community organizing. *Rules for Radicals* has been a playbook for community organizers since it was published in 1971, a year before his death. In ten lessons, he gave guidance on how to unite people into groups with power to bring about change. I have taught his methods to my classes since I began teaching in 1967.

In the 1930s, Alinsky began developing his methods in the slum neighborhoods surrounding Chicago's stockyards. After working with other South Side communities, he moved on to cities like Detroit and Oakland before returning to Chicago.

His method was to unite a community behind a common symbol, find an external enemy to unite against, then take direct action that causes conflict and brings the community's issues to the public's attention.

This quote gives a hint of Alinsky's controversial personality:

"Lest we forget at least an over-the-shoulder acknowledgment to the very first radical . . . the first radical known to man who rebelled against the establishment and did it so effectively that he at least won his own kingdom – Lucifer."[1]

Hillary Clinton wrote her senior thesis at Wellesley on Alinsky's work, and his influence on Jesse Jackson and Barack Obama is well-known. Groups ranging from 1960s radicals, to labor unions, to Tea Party conservatives have followed Alinsky's advice on how to organize themselves to gain power.

---

1   Saul David Alinsky, *Rules for Radicals* (New York: Random House, 1972).

© Marc PoKempner

Barack Obama's first campaign for political office, Chicago, 1995

25

THE MAKING OF BARACK OBAMA

*In politics, as in life, compromise has
both good and bad consequences.*

CHICAGO HAS MADE many national figures, most notably Hillary Clinton, Jesse Jackson, and, of course, Barack Obama. Our 44th president was molded by the city's blood-sport politics.

Barack first came to Chicago in 1985, an Alinsky-style community organizer come to the city where the method was invented. He worked the South Side, in Rosemont and other poor neighborhoods. Obama was drawn by the presence of Harold Washington, Chicago's first African-American mayor, the most progressive mayor in the country.

After leaving Chicago to attend Harvard Law School in 1988, Obama returned in 1991 with his shiny new law degree and set up shop with the civil rights and community development law firm of Davis, Miner, Barnhill, & Galland.[1]

---

1   I knew senior partner Jud Miner from the beginning of the Independent movement on Chicago's North Side. He had been corporation counsel for most of Mayor Washington's term. I worked with Jud as an expert witness in a series of race discrimination lawsuits which challenged the way ward boundaries were gerrymandered every decade to limit the number of blacks and Latino aldermen so whites could maintain control. Since Obama was not involved in those lawsuits, and I wasn't a witness in the civil rights suits that he handled, our paths did not intersect when he first returned to Chicago.

At the University of Chicago Law School, he rose from Fellow, to Lecturer, to Senior Lecturer. He quickly began working his way up the social and political ladder at a time when Mayor Richard M. Daley was firmly in control of the town, having begun his 22-year-term, the longest of any mayor in Chicago history.

Obama made his first major political move in 1995, when he successfully ran a campaign to defeat Alice Palmer, the incumbent Illinois state senator from the South Side district that ran through the Hyde Park, South Shore, and Chicago Lawn neighborhoods. He came under the tutelage of the African-American Senate President Emil Jones, who he had met as a community organizer, and who became a political godfather to this ambitious and talented new black politician. Emil allowed Obama to sponsor various pieces of key legislation, including important ethics legislation strongly supported by the good-government groups to which I belonged.

Barack then made a critical misstep, which still turned out well for him. In 2000, he ran for Congress against the popular 1st District African-American congressman, Bobby Rush. I wasn't involved on either side of that campaign, but friends who met Obama during the campaign found him to be arrogant and aloof. Obama's defeat had the effect of making him a better candidate and a better political tactician. And he learned to let his old community-organizer skills reassert themselves.

Obama's next big campaign was his 2003 run for the vacant U.S. Senate seat, which is when I first met him. I attended an IVI-IPO-sponsored debate of all 15 candidates in the Democratic primary. Among those running for that Senate seat were the sitting Illinois Comptroller, who had greater name recognition and a statewide office; a wealthy liberal lawyer with plenty of money to spend; and a state senator with the little-known and foreign-sounding name of Barack Obama.

Barack bested all the Democratic candidates in that first debate, demonstrating better, more knowledgeable, and more progressive positions on the issues of the day. I congratulated him afterwards, told him how well I thought he had done, and backed him publicly when IVI-IPO endorsed him.

I met up with him again soon afterwards, as his campaign unfolded and he began to be covered by national television. As he waited to be given an award from the Illinois Coalition for Political Reform for ethics legislation he had sponsored and passed with the help of Emil Jones' clout in Springfield, we got to spend a little social time together, before his other admirers and a national TV crew pulled him away for an interview.

Obama and I were not friends or colleagues in his Chicago days, although we had many connections in common and traveled in some of the same circles. For instance, I knew David Axelrod, one of his closest advisers, from when he was first a cub reporter at a small South Side community newspaper, and later a political reporter at the *Chicago Tribune*. I did not know Barack's wife Michele when she was a lawyer at a downtown firm or when she became an assistant to Mayor Daley and introduced Obama to him.

In Chicago, a fine political point is made of the difference between "independents," of which I am one, and "independent Democrats," which Obama is. In his Chicago years, this difference showed up when Obama essentially made an unspoken pact with Mayor Daley and the evolving political machine. Like Harold Washington in his early career before he split from the machine, Barack was free to pursue liberal and progressive policies in Springfield and Washington, D.C., as long as he didn't endorse local anti-machine candidates in Chicago or oppose the local party organization. He could offer ethics legislation to improve politics and government as corruption worsened in Illinois, but not take on Mayor Daley and his rubber-stamp City Council directly. Early in my political career, I made the other choice – to oppose machine politics in all its forms.

For President Obama, and probably for the country as well,

his pragmatic compromise worked and brought us a more progressive presidency than even the liberal Democrat Bill Clinton, who "triangulated" too many compromises with Republicans and the conservative wing of his own party. Certainly, the Chicago-trained President Obama was much more to my liking than the president who followed him.

There are splits and divisions in all political movements. For instance, there has always been a split between revolutionaries who want the violent overthrow of government, radicals who want fundamental change and may be willing to use some violence, and reformers who want substantial changes achieved non-violently.

Since World War II, Chicago liberals have been split between two camps. In one camp were the liberal or independent Democrats, including party members who generally voted with the party, but nevertheless did not support the Democratic machine that governed the city (and frequently the state). In the other camp were the "purer" Independents, who totally opposed the machine and were willing to support Republican candidates to get honest, efficient government and the reform of corrupt practices.

Liberal Democratic reform movements were led by people like Adlai Stevenson and Dawn Clark Netsch, while the Independent movement had its roots in the founding of the Independent Voters of Illinois during World War II and the Independent Precinct Organization after the 1968 Democratic National Convention. Alderman Leon Despres and I are examples of the Independent branch.

In modern times, the Independent movement has weakened. Both groups are now part of the reform movement inside the Democratic Party. Republicans have become more conservative, so progressives often cannot support their election. But we Independents also continue to fight against the local Democratic machine and run candidates against them.

Leon Despres, whom I nominated for an honorary degree at UIC

26

VISIONARY REFORMERS:
LEN, DAWN, RAY, & STUDS

*It takes backbone to fight for justice,
and no one does it alone.*

AT THE END of the 20th century, Leon Despres, Dawn Clark Netsch, Ray Nordstrand, and Studs Terkel were four giants in Chicago's reform movement. Their distinct backgrounds and personalities made them fascinating to work with. I owe these, and all my mentors, guides, and allies, a debt of gratitude.

Leon Despres

In a working-class town of broad shoulders and big mouths, Leon Despres stood out. He was, in my estimation, the best alderman to serve in the history of Chicago. A fierce Independent, he was one of the founders of the Independent Voters of Illinois (IVI) back in the 1940s.

Len, as his friends called him, was a tough labor lawyer and alderman from the mostly-black South Side 5th Ward in Hyde Park. He was elected in 1955, the same year Richard J. Daley became mayor. For the next twenty years they would be sparring partners in the fight over the future of the city.

With his vast experience, Len was a mentor to many reformers, including me. He taught me how to craft ordinances and budget amendments, how to speak in public and to the media, and how to hold press conferences. When I was first elected to the City Council in 1971, he taught me the ropes and organized our small group of Independent and Republican aldermen into a coalition with regular meetings and the chance to work together to introduce major legislative initiatives. With the occasional support of other aldermen, our group of seven formed the loyal opposition. Before our coalition was formed, Len sometimes had to stand alone fighting the machine in the City Council. After 1971, we were a legitimate voting bloc, upholding a different vision of what Chicago could be.

Len was aristocratic in his bearing. He spoke French, having spent time in Europe in his youth. His wife, Marian Despres, was herself a civic activist and an architectural preservationist. Len and Marian moved in activist and intellectual circles in Chicago and the world beyond. When Leon Trotsky was in exile in Mexico, they delivered clothes to him from supporters in the United States. While they were in Mexico, Diego Rivera painted Marian's portrait while Len and Frida Kahlo went to the movies.

Although Leon was white, a *Negro Digest* article in 1966 called him "the lone Negro spokesman in the Chicago City Council." The six black aldermen serving at the time were known to do the bidding of the powerful Boss Mayor Daley. But not Len. In Kenan Heise's fine book, *Chicago Afternoons with Leon*, he quotes Despres when he was 99 years old:

> *"At my age, I rejoice that Chicago has come as far as it has in regard to race. But people are still imprisoned by racial segregation in this city. Often – as in the past – it is an imprisonment based on where they are forced to live – in neighborhoods where there are no jobs, few opportunities, no good schools, no health facilities, no stores, no decent housing, no personal safety, and limited public transportation."*[1]

Throughout his life, Len fought against segregation and for progressive changes such as equal wages for women, the rights of labor unions, protection of open space, and positive urban planning. He did this not only while he was an alderman, but while he was City Council Parliamentarian under Mayors Byrne and Washington, on the Chicago Planning Commission to which he was appointed after his aldermanic career, and in his active law practice. Many of the reforms he proposed, which were initially voted down 49-1, are now law in Chicago.

Leon Despres received many awards and honorary degrees, including an honorary doctoral degree from University of Illinois at Chicago for which I was privileged to nominate him. Active throughout his life, he lived to be 101 years old. Len's old friend Studs Terkel spoke for all of us when he said, "I will take Leon Despres as 'my North Star,' a guide to ethics in government."

*   *   *   *   *

1   Kenan Heise, "Two Who Stood Up Against Racial Segregation in Chicago," *Chicago Afternoons with Leon: 99 ½ Years Old and Looking Forward* (Bloomington, IN: Author House, 2007), 76.

Dawn Clark Netsch

As a proud "lakefront liberal," Dawn Clark Netsch led an important branch of the reform movement in Illinois from the 1950s until her death in 2013. Stylish and distinctive as she puffed away on her long black cigarette holder, she could also be humorous and down-to-earth. For decades, we supported many of the same causes and shared the stage at community and political events.

Dawn got her political start supporting integration while she studied at Northwestern University. In the '40s and '50s, she worked as a volunteer in Adlai Stevenson II's campaigns for governor of Illinois and president of the United States.

I met Dawn in 1969 when I supported her campaign for Illinois Constitutional Convention delegate. After winning her election on Chicago's North Side, she and other independent delegates like Bernie Weisberg formed a key bloc within the Convention, making it possible to draft the most advanced state constitution in the country at the time. This was particularly true in areas like civil rights and home-rule revenue powers, for which Dawn was an advocate.

In 1972, I worked on Dawn's successful campaign to become an Illinois state senator. She became part of the "Crazy Eight" liberal senators who broke the stranglehold the Cook County Democratic machine held on the Senate. During those days, she and Richard M.

Daley were on opposite sides politically. She gave him the title "Dirty Little Richie" in those political battles, but endorsed him years later when he ran for mayor.

In 1990, Dawn was elected Illinois Comptroller as the first woman ever to win a statewide constitutional office in Illinois. The neon sign reading "Dawn Netsch, State Comptroller" still hangs proudly in the Northwestern Law School cafeteria in downtown Chicago.

Next, Dawn ran for governor against the moderate Republican incumbent, Jim Edgar. Although her "straight-shooter" pool-playing commercial garnered a lot of attention, she lost the election because she advocated increasing state taxes to fund education. But after his reelection, Governor Edgar adopted many of her proposals.

Not one to sit still, after her defeat Dawn co-founded the Illinois Campaign for Political Reform with Democrat U.S. Senator Paul Simon and Republican Lt. Governor Bob Kustra. To this day, it carries on the battle for ethics, campaign finance reform, and public funding of campaigns in Illinois.

Dawn was a trailblazer in many endeavors. She became a law professor at Northwestern University Law School at a time when only thirteen women had ever been law professors in the United States. She taught at Northwestern for over 40 years, and served on government reform commissions until her death. She had many friends, especially women she had mentored or had served as staffers on her campaigns or in government with her.

Dawn was a liberal Democrat, not a radical. She was not involved in the 1968 Democratic Convention and its polarizing sides. While she appeared at gay pride parades, she did not join peace marches. She was a fiscal conservative, but a social liberal. She was an intellectual who cared about the common people. She broke through the glass ceiling for women in law, academia, and politics. And she supported minority rights when many others did not. In the end, she became something like the patron saint of liberal Democrats in Illinois.

Dawn lived to be 86 years old and passed away in 2013.

Courtesy of Old Town School of Folk Music

Ray Nordstrand, General Manager of WFMT
and host of the folk music show "The Midnight Special"

Ray Nordstrand

Ray Nordstrand drew thousands of people into the world of classical music as the visionary general manager of WFMT, the country's foremost classical music station throughout the 20th century. But folk music was his true passion. He supported its revival and fostered the Chicago folk music scene for more than four decades. Much of his fame came from co-founding and hosting the "Midnight Special" program, filled with folk music and satire. Being featured and appearing on that live broadcast made the careers of many folk musicians.

Win Stracke founded the Old Town School of Folk Music, but Ray was its great supporter throughout his life. As he grew older and was confined to a wheelchair, he enjoyed the school's concerts from his cabaret table to the right of the stage. Performers would regularly give a shout out to thank him for helping make their careers and advancing the folk music tradition. Many of his friends, myself included, would greet him as he held court at his table during intermission.

Ray made an often-overlooked contribution to Chicago's political history. After the 1968 Democratic National Convention, most civic and business leaders were afraid to oppose City Hall and Mayor Richard J. Daley's iron rule. A number of Chicago actors, musicians, and performers were fellow liberals and radicals, but few of the heads of mainstream media backed our calls for reform for fear of retribution from City Hall and the political machine. But Ray had the courage to stand up and be counted with us. By marrying the worlds of folk music and political reform, Ray became one of the fathers of progressive change in Chicago.

During the years I was a reform alderman, Ray pulled together and hosted fundraisers like my tongue-in-cheek "Valentine to City Hall" on Valentine's Day at the old Quiet Knight folk club on Belmont Avenue. Comedians did irreverent parodies and impersonations of "da mayor" with his broken syntax, and folk singers sang protest and political songs like Win Stracke's "The 43rd Ward," which made fun of 43rd Ward boss and Alderman Paddy Baler.

The shows were so controversial at City Hall that Richard Harding, the owner of the Quiet Knight, almost lost his liquor license because of the events held there. Under Ray's leadership, however, we continued to hold folk music and satire benefits throughout my eight years as alderman. They were a highlight of my aldermanic career and the cultural wars to reform Chicago. For in addition to providing campaign funds, they also merged the cultural and political movements to end racial segregation and the Vietnam War, and to begin empowering citizens in boss-run Chicago.

Ray also put together the entertainment at the 44th Ward Fairs that involved thousands of people in celebrating the cultural diversity and talent of our Lake View community. He brought in the best talent that Chicago had to offer, including Steve Goodman, Bonnie Kolac, and Ed and Fred Holstein. Sarajane and I were always amazed at the acts that signed up to perform. But as she told me, "Nobody says 'no' to Ray!"

There was a good reason nobody said "no" to Ray. He was unselfish, and much more interested in promoting his community and city than himself. If he was willing to work on a community event and host a performer on his radio program, neither the performers nor anyone else could turn down his request to appear, to help, and to join together to build a better Chicago. Ray left us too soon in 2005, at the age of 72.

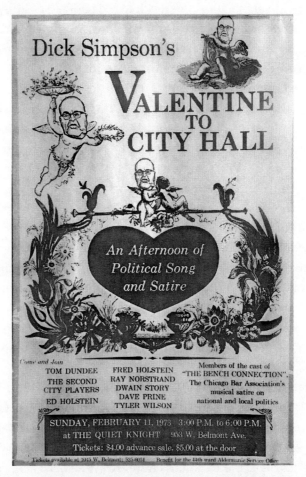

Poster for my first aldermanic office benefit, 1971

© Robert Kameczura

Studs Terkel as an MC at a fundraiser in my second congressional campaign, 1996

Studs Terkel

Ray's sidekick and compatriot at WFMT was Studs Terkel. The last time I saw Studs was at political guru and journalist Don Rose's 2007 New Year's Eve party. He died on Halloween, 2008, three years after Ray's passing.

After being blacklisted in the McCarthy era, Studs started his famous radio program "The Studs Terkel Show" on WFMT in 1952. On the air more than four decades, it led to his famous oral history books. In his biography of Studs, Alan Wieder wrote that "his commitment to conversation was in effect a quest for justice . . . Studs' interviews . . . did not just provide a microphone for the voiceless. Instead, he taught interviewees as well as his listeners and readers that we were not impotent, that we had much to say, and that our voices and our

---

actions, not a savior politician, could change the world."[1]

Studs knew how to tell a compelling story with his raspy, penetrating voice. He always wore his trademark red-checkered shirt and red socks, and I happen to know that he was something of a klutz, especially with electronic devices. I often marveled that he was able to operate the famous mic and tape recorder with which he chronicled the stories of the rich and the poor, but especially the voiceless.

His friend, Chicago journalist Mike Royko, knew well Studs' ability to get at deeper truths in his interviews and conversations. He said of him, "he knows where their heart is, he knows where their soul is, and where to find the things in them they care about."[2] Both on air and in print, Studs revealed our age, our era, and our stories to ourselves – even if it got him blacklisted and kicked off television.

Studs' wife Ida was also a visionary cultural leader. As his biographer put it, "They sang the same songs."[3] They loved theater, politics, and music, and shared a joint commitment to cherish and improve the world – especially for those who had few other champions.

When I was 44th Ward alderman, Studs and Ida lived in my ward and became ardent supporters. Ida was herself a major political activist and participated in innumerable political demonstrations while Studs and I shared the platform speaking.

I was a guest on Studs' radio show three times over the years. The routine was the same each time: the program was taped live at 10 am, after which we would go around the corner to Riccardo's Restaurant for lunch and more conversation. Folks there would come over to greet us – or more accurately, to greet Studs.

His mind still sharp until the very end, Studs passed away in 2008 at the age of 96.

---

1   Alan Wieder, *Studs Terkel: Politics, Culture, but Mostly Conversation* (New York: Monthly Review Press, 2016), 12, 19.

2   Originally quoted in Tony Parker, *Studs Terkel: A Life in Words* (New York: Henry Holt and Company, 1996). Also quoted in Wieder, 32

3   Wieder, 35.

IT HAS BEEN a privilege to know Len, Dawn, Ray, and Studs, and to know that our efforts have been about more than just politics, movements, and demonstrations. They have been in service of a social and culture war, and not just the one narrowly defined by political correctness. We joined together using radio, books, music, and battles with City Hall to amplify the voices of the unheard.

In 2010, the Supreme Court handed down a landmark ruling on the *Citizens United v. Federal Election Commission* case. The Court held that, because of the right to freedom of speech, the government cannot restrict independent political expenditures by corporations, labor unions, and other associations. We have been suffering the fallout of that decision ever since.

Shortly before the 2008 Democratic primary, Citizens United, a conservative non-profit organization, had wanted to air a film critical of Hillary Clinton. This violated a federal statute prohibiting electioneering communications near an election. The Supreme Court found that law to be in conflict with the U.S. Constitution and its guarantee of freedom of political speech.

In its groundbreaking ruling, the Court not only allowed electioneering communications by corporations and labor unions, but also allowed "independent expenditures" by them as well. The true effect of this and later court decisions was to open the floodgates to more money in elections and the proliferation of Super PACs which could legally hide the names of their donors. Decades of efforts to reform campaign finance have been undermined by wrong-headed court decisions since 2010.

Voting in Sierra Leone, 1966

27

ELECTIONS AND THE ART
OF CAREFUL POLITICS

Bend, but don't break.

ELECTIONS HAVE MAJOR consequences for our lives, both individually and collectively. Without them, there would be no way to enforce the will of "we, the people." In our representative democracy, it is both a right and responsibility for citizens of every socioeconomic background to have a say in who will represent us and our opinions.

Elections also give us the opportunity to hear the issues of the day being debated and discussed. We are free to be involved in the process as much or as little as we wish, but the responsibility for the quality of our leaders rests with us, the voters.

That is why I have spent dozens of election days watching polls, traveling to troubled polling spots, and answering troubleshooting phone calls at campaign headquarters. While I was a sitting alderman, I was even briefly arrested for preventing electioneering at a polling place in a hotly-contested election, until the assistant state's attorneys arrived and released me. It is to our detriment that more than half of us fail to vote in elections – especially local elections. I can only think this because we have not fully understood what was at stake. Without free, fair, and vigorously-contested elections, democracy fails. And there is no doubt in my mind that our democracy is in peril.

To be fair, there are flaws in our system. First of all, elections have gotten too expensive. Especially since the *Citizens United* court decision, it simply costs too much to run for higher public office. It is more difficult than ever for candidates to raise huge sums without selling out to wealthy individuals or powerful interest groups. That is why I continually advocate for public funding of elections. I am convinced now that it, along with other election reforms, is the only way to reclaim our democracy.

For example, 2014 was the most expensive non-presidential, off-year election in Illinois history up until that time, with more than $60 million raised in the gubernatorial election alone. In 2018, we are expecting the multi-candidate gubernatorial race to cost more than $100 million, since we have several millionaires and billionaires running. In our state's contested congressional elections, candidates spent between $2 and $4 million each in the suburban districts in 2014 and 2016. On the other hand, most of our state-level legislative districts had almost no contest because of how the districts have been gerrymandered in the flawed redistricting process.

Thus, gerrymandering is the second huge flaw that needs to be reformed. Elected officials currently choose the voters rather than the voters choosing their elected officials. The reelection rate of incumbents in Congress is more than 90 percent. It is similar for incumbents at the state and local level.

Thirdly, we are in a period of extreme partisanship, especially at the national level. True, we've experienced other periods in American history when parts of the government haven't worked well and divisions have been very partisan. We were more divided politically during the Civil War; we almost fell apart during the Great Depression when socialism and communism were on the rise until the election of Franklin Roosevelt. At the end of the 1960s, the country was again very divided, and there were protests in the streets. In 1974, President Nixon was even forced to resign the presidency to avoid being impeached and convicted. So although ours is not the worst partisan era in our nation's history, that doesn't excuse how bad things are today. Extreme partisanship must be tamed.

Sometimes vetoing, demonstrating, protesting, and saying no loudly and emphatically is what we have to do. I learned that back in the civil rights and antiwar movements of the 60s. But what we seem to have forgotten is that it is possible to compromise on most legislative issues and to support less-than-perfect political candidates and still advance our cause.

Coming out of the 2014 elections, Republicans controlled both the House and the Senate and gridlock became the pattern in Washington. Obama was able to get things done only by creative use of executive orders. In 2016, America voted in a Republican president and the Republicans maintained a majority in both houses of Congress, although by only a 52-48 majority in the Senate. Now each party is far less willing to afford "courtesies" to the other side as in the past. "Reaching across the aisle" is a disappearing art.

Everyone is in protective mode. Moderate Republicans worry about primary challenges from the Tea Party and President Trump's supporters, causing the Republican Party to move to the right. Democrats, for their part, demonize Republicans and worry about attacks from their left, more progressive wing. Even though many members of Congress get along with each other on a personal level, they are held captive by the more-extreme views of their constituencies. Bernie Sanders' influence is felt on one side, and the radical right on the other. From many liberal Democrats' point of view, people who would even consider working with President Trump to reach a compromise and govern are nearly traitors.

Both parties use parliamentary tricks on each other. In past American history, people might not have liked a filibuster, but they put up with it rather than destroy the Senate. It remained a right, to be used only as a last resort. But now that's been thrown out the window, and we have total political war – even though in private both parties would probably be content to make some sort of peace.

No one wants to compromise their vision of a better future. But speaking as a progressive, there are things about the Republican vision of the future that are quite correct, such as term limits on elected officials. We should be able to admit that. Where we can, we should allow the other side half a loaf, if that's what it takes to keep the government functioning, rather than destroying the country along the way. In fact, there is room to cooperate on a great many things. On principles of good government such as campaign finance reform. On not having race wars. On closing tax loopholes. On having a sensible, reasonable budget. On not doing stupid things like eating our seed corn. We need to find common ground – we need to govern.

How do we do this? When our party isn't in power, we need to be the loyal opposition. Loyal to the nation, and loyal to ourselves. But instead, we too often choose absolute opposition. It's as if the hidden agenda is to make things as bad as possible so the people will most certainly join the revolution to come. For the sake of the republic, we need to stop doing that. There is strength in coming to a compromise with the Republicans on some things, and on some issues. And Republicans have to compromise with us on some issues, like civil rights, where we are correct.

We need to think long term. The short-term result of not compromising, and the downward spiral that it causes, may help Democrats in the next election. We may even gain both houses of Congress. But the enormous amount of money that both sides will have spent demonizing each other, "crossing the line" in what we say about each other, will have the effect of making most Americans completely disgusted with both sides. Remember, the greatest effect of negative advertising is suppression of the vote; citizens decide that all politicians are crooks and decide to withdraw altogether. Yet, we the people, the "demos," must be involved in elections and public life if there is to be democracy.

Holding onto our view of the future while cooperating for the good of the nation isn't easy to do. It requires a very careful calibration, balancing what's legitimate opposition with what needs to be done to keep the government going, to keep the American people whole. We must think long term. What I am describing here, this kind of careful, principled politics – this is the essence of our representative democracy.

All of that being said, it is also important to promote deliberative or participatory democracy. More of that must be done, and in a thoughtful and responsible way. People want to believe that they can make a difference and that their lives matter. They need a sense that elections matter, that what they do politically as citizens matters. I forever urge reclaiming democracy, giving more "power to the people." But we, the people, can only have a right to control our government if we are informed and active.

At Passover Seders, there is always a happy part of the meal in which we sing the song "Dayenu." The Hebrew word means "it would have been enough."

In fifteen upbeat verses, this thousand-year-old song tells us that it would have been enough if God had only freed the Jews from Egyptian slavery. It would have been enough if he had done the miracles that saved them in the wilderness. It would have been enough if God had given them the Torah. Any one of these miracles would have been enough and a clear cause for celebration. But the fact that God caused *all* of this to happen is truly joyous.

And so it is with me. My life has reached a stage where I can say "Dayenu," it would have been enough. And yet, to my surprise, my story still includes new beginnings.

Fighting the good fight in Chicago City Hall, 1971

28

THE GOOD FIGHT

Take it from an old Eagle Scout: Be Prepared.

IN LATE 2015, just before my 76th birthday, the leaders of a small election reform group named Who's Counting? - Chicago asked me to apply for an opening on the Chicago Board of Election Commissioners. I updated my CV, gathered recommendation letters, and filed my application, in which I declared: *"I am concerned with the challenges facing the conduct of elections and with the need to encourage greater citizen participation today..."*

A week before Christmas, I met with Cook County Chief Judge Tim Evans, the man who would nominate and select the candidate, to be confirmed by a vote of all the judges. I had known Tim since our days in the City Council together back in the 1970s, and had supported him in his bid to replace Harold Washington after Washington's death. As Tim and I talked, I stressed that I had many qualifications after 50 years of teaching and political involvement, and multiple ideas on how to help with the voting board's challenges. All the voting machines would soon need to be replaced without federal funding to help, the city and county election commissions should be merged, and the problem of voter apathy, especially among the young, had to be overcome.

In the end, I didn't get appointed. Once again, I proved to be too radical. But since I believe that we are defined by what we dare to do, I am glad I applied, and hope to continue to serve my city and my country.

IT IS GOOD to still be in the game, teaching, organizing, protesting. Not like the glory days of my youth, but doing my part by sending books to Sierra Leone, raising money for Chicago Shakespeare, joining the North Side Housing and Supportive Services in their effort to end homelessness in Chicago, supporting the resistance movement in this turbulent political era. And with over 100 media interviews a year, I can still help shape the stories that change people's minds.

There are also some victories, both political and nonpolitical, from which I draw encouragement. For instance, I recently attended the opening of "The Yard," Chicago Shakespeare's amazing third theater. Now a world-renowned theater company, Chicago Shakespeare is a far cry from its modest beginnings 30 years ago, when Sarajane performed Henry V on the roof of the Red Lion Pub and I served on the first board of directors.

On the other hand, as with most people my age, I am increasingly aware of losses and change. Some of my favorite restaurants have closed: the Lincoln restaurant, an old-time North Center landmark on Lincoln Avenue; La Bocca della Verita, the wonderful Roman restaurant in Lincoln Square; and Cyrano's, a French bistro on North Wells Street. In Lakeview, the wacky toy and pop-culture store Uncle Fun closed when owner Ted Frankel retired and moved to Baltimore. Jewelers Row, the center of small jewelry stores that sat on Wabash Avenue for over a century, seems in danger of disappearing entirely. And after all these years, I still miss the old Hull House neighborhood and the Maxwell Street market which was displaced by UIC.

I miss the friends and colleagues I've lost, in ever-increasing numbers as the years pass. Friends like Bob Houston, Leon Despres, and Fred Hess. Remembering them, I move between melancholy and gratitude. The whole generation that came of age in the 1960s or before is now passing away.

But despite divorces, deaths, and disappointments in my life, I count myself lucky. Blessings have far outweighed tragedies. I have felt the winds of history and known first-hand people who changed our world. Friends have made me wiser and more self-aware. The women in my life have given me a family, taught me about friendship, and loved me with my faults. My children, Kate and August Donley, my son-in-law Jeff Olson, and especially my granddaughters, Lilian and Paula, provide much of the inspiration, reason, and support necessary for my life. My hope is that their lives will outshine mine.

Of the four main dimensions to my life, politics, love, religion, and teaching, it is teaching that has been my mainstay. Above all, I am a teacher, whether in the classroom, on TV, or in political battles. I have taught thousands of students the importance of civic engagement and been proud of what they have done to make the world better. Even in my next book, *Democracy's Rebirth*, I will be teaching as I recount the flaws of democracy in the U.S., in Africa, and in Chicago, and argue for a more deliberative and participatory form of democracy than we have now.

In my personal life, I have fallen in love again. I spend more time in Vermont with my partner Margaret England and close family. I am selling the building in Chicago in which Sarajane, my son, August, and I have lived, and am downsizing to a smaller apartment. I have new projects underway at the university. Overall, I've experienced life and love in abundance. I have been blessed, and it has been enough.

AFTER ALL THESE years, what have I learned about the progressive fight to achieve democracy and justice? I've learned that, while social and economic forces affect politics and government, real change is primarily determined by political actions, political history, and political choices. I've learned that you cannot start at the top, elect a president, and work your way down. Change has to start at the grassroots, and we have to be ready to make it happen. I've learned that democracy requires conflict in which the final appeal is to the people. Fine-sounding pronouncements are not enough. We have to run for office, propose legislation, attend community, civic, and political meetings, and join with others to accomplish political goals. Sometimes we have to protest, and sometimes we are the government. Either way, we have to recognize opportunities, and be ready to move quickly when they arrive.

My generation thought it would be easy to make the world better. We figured it would only take a few years, and then we would be done and could retire to our private lives. But it was much harder than we imagined. There is enormous evil in the world, and each of us is flawed. But there is also basic goodness which can be tapped into, if we have the faith to do so. If we are ready.

It is amazing to me that our republic has lasted for more than 200 years, despite depressions, riots, uprisings, and wars – even our terrible Civil War. This hasn't happened by accident. It has been a fight the whole way.

So, it looks like we have one more political hurrah before my generation passes on. A number of us still remain in the fight to win more progressive policies and revitalize our democracy. We have been privileged to fight for a better world in our lifetimes. Now we pass on to future generations, not a completed transformation, but a work in progress. We ask you to do your part. Keep the faith. Fight the good fight.

Seeing life in 3D with my granddaughter Lilian

ACKNOWLEDGMENTS

THIS MEMOIR BEGAN as 60 vignettes of op-ed length, produced over the course of a year or so. At my friend Anna Perlberg's book launch, I met Nancy Sayre of Golden Alley Press who agreed to publish my book. It has been decades since I have had a hands-on editor, and a memoir is a very different thing from the textbooks and monographs that I usually publish, so I have appreciated Nancy's editorial guidance. In addition, her husband, Michael, has designed a handsome book.

My partner, Margaret England, served as a critical beta reader, correcting many problems in the original manuscript. Tom Gradel, my friend of 40 years, helped with some corrections and with promotion of the book. Scott Simpson corrected some of the dates which I had confused.

Thousands of supporters, allies, and students created the stories which I retell here. I have always been part of a movement, and this is in many ways the story of my generation, not just my personal story.

Thanks also to my family, Kate and August Donley, Jeff Olson, and my granddaughters Lilian and Paula Olson, who make life worth living. I thought they should know more of their step-father and grandfather.

For all of you who have given help and encouragement, I am grateful. Any mistakes which remain are solely mine, but there are fewer than there would have been without you.

CREDITS

EXCEPT AS NOTED below, all images are courtesy of the author. Grateful acknowledgement is made to the following individuals and institutions for permission to reprint images:

Chapter 6

Red Square and the Kremlin Wall, Photograph. Brorson, 1960s, SAS Scandinavian Airlines, http://images.flysas.com. Public Domain.

Chapter 8

"Mayor Daley at the 1968 Chicago Democratic National Convention": *Illinois delegates at the Democratic National Convention of 1968, Chicago Mayor Daley heckling Senator Ribicoff*, Photograph. Warren K. Leffler, 8-28-68, Library of Congress, U.S. News & World Report collection, http://www. loc.gov/pictures/item/2012647951/. Public Domain.

"Bobby We Miss You": photo still from *Conventions: The Land Around Us*, Film (Chicago: University of Illinois at Chicago, 1969).

Chapter 9

"Campaigning for Bernie Weisberg": photo still from *By the People: A Study of Independent Politics*, Film (Chicago: University of Illinois at Chicago, 1970).

"Fr. Carl Lezak": photo still from *By the People: A Study of Independent Politics*, Film (Chicago: University of Illinois at Chicago, 1970).

"Bernie Weisberg": photo still from *By the People: A Study of Independent Politics*, Film (Chicago: University of Illinois at Chicago, 1970).

Chapter 14

"1960s protest": *Anti-war demonstration before 1968 Democratic National Convention in Chicago*, Photograph. David Wilson, 8-10-68, https://www.flickr.com/photos/david-wilson1949/6056934707/. (CC BY 2.0)

Chapter 15

"Declaring the Wellington Avenue UCC Nuclear Free Zone": Newsgroup Chicago, Inc., 1984/photo by Al Podgorski

"With my mother at my Wellington ordination ceremony": photo credit: William Mahin

"Guatemalan refugees with Rev. David Cheverie": © Noel Neuburger

Chapter 16

"Encouraging political engagement" photo credit: Scott Braam

Chapter 17

"Mayor Harold Washington on the campaign trail": © Marc PoKempner

Chapter 19

"Our official campaign photo": © Susan Reich

Chapter 20

"With Carol Moseley Braun": © Roberta Dupuis-Devlin, UIC

Chapter 21

"Sarajane Avidon and other cast members of Chicago
Shakespeare Theater": photo courtesy of Chicago
Shakespeare Theater

Chapter 24

School of Athens, Painting. Raphael, 1511, Wikimedia Commons
[http://commons.wikimedia.org/wiki/Image:Sanzio_01.jpg]
this is a cropped version. {PD-Art} Public Domain.

Chapter 25

"Barack Obama's first campaign": © Marc PoKempner

Chapter 26

"Leon Despres": © Roberta Dupuis-Devlin, UIC
Dawn Clark Netsch, Photograph. Author unknown, date
unknown, source Abraham Lincoln Presidential Library,
Springfield, Illinois, ALPLM Oral History Program, Illinois
Statecraft Project, Legislators Series. Public Domain.
"Ray Nordstrand": photo courtesy of Old Town School
of Folk Music
"Studs Terkel": © Robert Kameczura

Chapter 28

"Fighting the good fight": © 1971 All rights reserved. Distributed
by Tribune Content Agency, LLC

Cover photographic credits:

Front cover: © 1971 All rights reserved. Distributed by Tribune
Content Agency, LLC
Back cover photograph of the author: © Roberta Dupuis-Devlin,
UIC

INDEX

ABOUT THE AUTHOR

DICK SIMPSON is a former Chicago alderman, an expert on Chicago politics and elections, and a longtime professor of political science. He is devoted to advancing the cause of participatory politics and social justice in Chicago, where he continues to oppose the power of the political machine.

Dick Simpson can be reached at
dick.simpson@goldenalleypress.com

CPSIA information can be obtained
at www.ICGtesting.com
Printed in the USA
LVOW12s0115120518
576963LV00001B/38/P